everyday KITCHEN for kids

In memory of my father,
who could make the most
marvellous things out of
seemingly nothing

everyday
K·I·T·C·H·E·N
for kids

100 amazing savoury and sweet recipes
children can really make

jennifer low

photography by ryan szulc

Grub Street • London

Published in 2014 by

Grub Street

4 Rainham Close

London

SW11 6SS

Email: food@grubstreet.co.uk

Web: www.grubstreet.co.uk

Twitter: @grub_street

Text copyright © Jennifer Low 2012

First published in Canada in 2012 by Whitecap Books

Editors: Lana Okerlund and Theresa Best

Design: Michelle Furbacher

Food photography: Ryan Szulc

Food and prop styling: Jennifer Low

A CIP catalogue record for this book is available from the British Library

ISBN 978-1-909808-04-1

The information in this book is true and complete to the best of the

author's knowledge. All recommendations are made without guarantee

on the part of the author or Grub Street. The author and the publisher

disclaim any liability in connection with the use of this information.

Printed and bound in Malta

contents

Introduction and Acknowledgements 7 ● Dear Kids 9 ● Dear Parents, Guardians, and Other Helpers 11 Organising the Kitchen for Kids 12 ● Cook's Glossary 15

YOUR RESTAURANT MENU 21

Cook a delicious main or side dish to help with the family meal!

French Toast in a Pan [*breakfast*] 22

Good Morning Bacon! [*breakfast*] [GF] 24

Batch o' Brekkie Sausages [*breakfast*] [GF] 26

Cashew Couscous (Bless You!) [*side dish*] 27

Roasted Tomato and Bocconcini Salad [*side dish*] [GF] 28

Feast Rice [*side dish*] [GF] 31

Simple Rice and Peas [*side dish*] [GF] 32

Cinnamon Baby Carrots [*side dish*] [GF] 33

Baker's Dozen Chive Biscuits [*side dish*] 35

Smashed Mini Potatoes [*side dish*] [GF] 36

Upside-Down Baked Potatoes [*side dish*] [GF] 38

Buttered Green Beans [*side dish*] [GF] 40

Parmesan Risotto [*side dish*] [GF] 41

Rice, Orzo, and Split Pea Trio [*side dish*] 43

Unfried Picnic Chicken Drumsticks [*main*] [GF] 44

Beef Stew Ooh-La-La [*main*] [GF] 47

Coconut-Curry Kookoo Chicken [*main*] [GF] 48

Lasagne Jumble [*main*] 51

Mozzarella Chicken [*main*] [GF] 52

Seven Seas Salmon [*main*] [GF] 55

Every-Flavour Pork Chops [*main*] [GF] 56

Your Own BBQ-Sauced Chicken [*main*] [GF] 59

YOUR KITCHEN SPECIALS 61

Make your favourite meals and snacks just the way you like them!

Cocoa-Kissed Banana Oatmeal [*breakfast*] 63

Piggies in Blankets [*lunch*] 64

Real Mac 'n' Cheddar Cheese [*lunch or supper*] 66

Spinach and Mushroom Frittata [*lunch or supper*] [GF] 69

Hula Hawaiian Pizza [*lunch or supper*] 70

Hocus Pocus Pizza [*lunch or supper*] [GF] 72

Gobble-Up Turkey Burgers [*lunch or supper*] [GF] 74

Lovin' Oven Hamburgers [*lunch or supper*] [GF] 76

Burger Buns [*lunch or supper*] 78

Fin-Tastic Fish Fillets [*supper*] [GF] 80

Really Big Chicken Meatballs [*supper*] [GF] 83

Lettuce Wraps with Crumbled Asian Pork [*supper*] [GF] 85

Tangy Chicken Wings [*snack*] [GF] 86

Soft Twisted Pepperoni Breadsticks [*snack*] 88

Munchy Crunchy Crackers [*snack*] 90

Tortilla Corn Chips [*snack*] [GF] 93

Parmesan Puffs [*snack*] [GF] 96

NOTE [GF] *means recipe is gluten-free. (See page 17.)*

YOUR OWN BAKERY 99

Be a pastry chef! Dazzle everyone with amazing breads, cakes, and pies!

Fresh Lemon Cupcakes 100
Fresh Lemon Double-Glaze [GF] 102
Sugared Doughnut Puffs 103
Chocolate Banana Loaf 105
Warm Chocolate Brioches 107
Little Fresh Blueberry Pies 109
Pecan Sweetie Pies 112
Rainy Day Banana Bread [GF] 114
O.J. Glaze [GF] 115
Blueberry Sunshine Muffins [GF] 116
Apricot Scoop Cake 119
Little Black Forest Cake 120
Pink Cherry Cake 122
Pink Cloud Frosting [GF] 124
Cocoa Buttercream Frosting [GF] 124

TIPS ON FROSTING CAKES 125

Surprising Chocolate Cake 127
Vanilla Velvet Cake [GF] 128
Vanilla Cream Frosting [GF] 130
Fudgy Frosting [GF] 130
Frosting Fudge [GF] 131
Dark Chocolate Cake [GF] 133
Feta Focaccia Bread 134
Champion Ciabatta 136
Whole Wheat Sandwich Bread 138
Cheddar Egg Bread 140
Tomato Salsa Cornbread 142
Spring Onion Bread 143
Cheese Pizza Muffins 144

YOUR COOKIE JAR 147

Bake a cookie for every kind of craving!

Chocolate Chippers 149
Cinnamoons 151
Peek-a-Pokes 153
Old-Fashioned Sugar Cookies 154
Glossy Cookie Glaze [GF] 156
Sweet Date Pockets 157
Cocoa Cranberry Crack-Ups 160
Dark Chocolate Crisps 163
Finnigans 164
Cookie Tortoises [GF] 167
Nuterettis [GF] 168
Sugar Delights [GF] 170
Chocolate Rondelles [GF] 173
Brown Sugar Crinkles [GF] 174
Peanut Butter Beezies [GF] 175

YOUR SWEET TREATS 177

Make delightfully unique goodies for your sweet tooth!

Almond-Oat Baked Apples 179
Peaches in Pastry Nests 180
Apple Crisp 182
Fruit Fritters [GF] 185
Warm Caramel Banana Sundaes [GF] 186
Fresh Berry Shortcakes 188
Whoopie Pies 190
Whoopie Pie Filling [GF] 192
Sponge Toffee Lollipops [GF] 193
Buttery Granola Bars 197
Hazelnut Fudge Pebbles [GF] 198
Double-Chocolate Brownies 200
Classic Brownie Frosting [GF] 203
Mint Brownie Frosting [GF] 203
Fudgelicious Brownies [GF] 204
Custards in a Warm Bath [GF] 206
Tirami-Moo 208
Cheesecake Mousse and Cookie Parfaits 210

Index 212

Introduction and Acknowledgements

Several years ago I wrote *Kids Kitchen*, this book's predecessor. I developed recipes for children that used only simple kitchen tools and were in small, manageable stages. Electrical appliances weren't even required! All manner of culinary whizbang had become possible. *Kids Kitchen* became an international bestseller and families now think of it as the "real" cookbook for children. Kids I meet can proudly recite the names of the recipes they made. It is remarkable.

I'm sure this book, *Everyday Kitchen for Kids*, will also find its enthusiastic fans. In the past few years, I've been testing new recipe ideas I know kids will love. This book is a collection of the best ones. It has a larger roster of savoury recipes than the first book because children love cooking for the family table. But there's also a grand selection of sweet goodies for kids to create on lazy days at home.

Every delicious recipe is photographed. As in the first book, none of the recipes requires children to use electrical appliances, sharp knives, or the stovetop. Safety comes first so kids can truly take charge. They're so proud of the recipes they make!

Everyday Kitchen for Kids is the culmination of a dedicated and enthusiastic team:

THE INSPIRATION. I'm lucky enough to travel through life with my own funny little tribe, my husband, John, and my kids, Lee and Livvy. They're my loves and my world. I think they were as excited to see this book come together as I was. They informally tested dishes and gamely brainstormed recipe names. My kids told me bluntly when a recipe wouldn't fly and patted me on the back when I tweaked one for the better. The book was often a family collaboration and we had fun with every minute of it!

THE BELIEVERS. Every book must have its champions behind the scenes. My dear friend Robert McCullough always kept this title at the top of his publishing agenda—and close to his heart. The team at my publisher never compromised on the quality required to make this book the standout they hoped for.

THE BEAUTY MERCHANTS. Photographer Ryan Szulc captured just the right balance of beauty and playfulness in every image. He managed the epic shoot with grace and good humour. And if ever a crumb fell astray, photo assistant Matt Gibson wielded his brand of invisible digital magic. Then pictures and words sprang to life under the keen eye of art director Michelle Furbacher.

THE WORDSMITHS. A recipe only works as well as its words, numbers, and logic dictate. With the expert guidance of book editor Lana Okerlund and Theresa Best, no detail was too small to polish. They helped create a whole new lexicon for a book to capture the imagination of its young audience.

THE MUM NETWORK. Sometimes it takes a mum to get the job done right—in this case, several of them. Shirley Chow, Jen Haverty, and Charmaine Underwood-Graham went beyond the call of duty, testing recipes with their kids and inviting other families to get involved. Also, a huge hurrah for my kitchen assistant, Sarah Wallace. She powered through recipe after recipe during shoots without ever breaking a sweat, which is why she wins the award for "Most Organised Person on the Planet."

THE ULTIMATE TESTERS. Of course, a heartfelt thank you to the wonderful kid cooks who measured and mixed every recipe with such care. I was inspired by your uncompromising quest for the best. Only recipes kids enjoyed eating and could make themselves made it into this book. A big thank you goes to my kitchen gang:

Abby Barnes
Paige and Laiken Bell
Chloe and Jennifer Braun
Riley Burstyn
Sydney Chan
Max and Quinn Chow
Kaia, Tasi, Jasper, and Bria Darke
Bronwyn Stella Davies
Jessie Drzewicki
Weston and Hannah Farnworth
Jade and Julia "Boo" Graham
John, Thomas, Daniel, and Laura Hunter
Megan Jones
Lucy and Ava Low
Amanda and Ariel Mackintosh

Leigha Maerten
Milo and Emmett Mighdoll
Kaitlyn, Megan, and Rebecca Moffat
Kayla and Hannah Raymond
Sofia and Ella Rimando
Lars Scott
Aaron Stafford
Ava Stechey
Tehya Wass-Gardner
Paisha Watkins
Jessica Wilson

Thank you to everyone for helping to make this book so special!

Jennifer Low

Dear Kids

You are about to go on an adventure you'll never forget. You're going to make recipes that are delicious to eat and that will amaze your family and friends!

Everyday Kitchen for Kids has 100 recipes created just for you. You'll be excited to discover you can make your own hamburgers, pizza as good or better than ones you order, chicken in all kinds of scrumptious flavours, bread that looks like it came straight from the fancy bakery, the best brownies, lovely types of cakes, and lots more. The list of choices is wonderfully long.

As you get started, ask an adult helper to stay nearby to lend a hand or explain anything you're unclear about. Your dishes will turn out best if you read the whole recipe before you begin to cook. Check that you have all the ingredients and supplies that are listed. You don't want to get to the middle of a recipe and find out you're missing something important.

It's also a good idea to read Organising the Kitchen for Kids (page 12) before you begin. And after you choose a recipe to make, you can look up anything in it you don't understand in the Cook's Glossary (page 15).

When you're cooking, don't rush. Follow each step carefully so you don't skip anything. But don't worry about making everything absolutely perfect, either. Just because a bread is a funny shape doesn't make it any less delicious. And if you get a slightly different number of cookies or muffins than the recipe says, that's okay, too. Cooking is fun!

There are five chapters to choose from. You can cook recipes for family meals, snacks to share with brothers, sisters or friends, or all kinds of sweet treats, too. Take a look at the photos and pick out your favourites.

And keep in mind that when your recipe is baking or chilling, you can help clean up. Even if you're too young to do the dishes, you can still put dirty bowls and tools by the sink. Keeping tidy is an important part of cooking. Besides, if you don't make a mess, your helper is more likely to help you cook again soon.

When your recipe is ready to eat, don't forget to share it. Then you can enjoy each and every bite and be proud that you were the chef who made it!

Happy cooking!

Jennifer Low

Dear Parents, Guardians, and Other Helpers

It's about the doing.

The best part about *Everyday Kitchen for Kids* is that the recipes are specially designed for children to do most of the cooking themselves. This means kids don't cut with sharp knives, work with electrical appliances, or stand over a hot stove. They don't need to. All they require are simple tools (like a wooden spoon, whisk, or kitchen scissors) to turn out delicious main dishes and treats. Kids also love that every recipe is photographed so they can easily visualise the end results.

It took many, many tests to get the child-friendly recipes just right. Dozens of children also tested them. I kept only the ones they raved over.

Before cooking, it's important for you to read the child's selected recipe, the Organising the Kitchen for Kids chapter, and entries in the Cook's Glossary pertinent to the chosen recipe. After the cooking begins, adult supervision is always advised, but you're there mainly to supervise, and perhaps pull a dish from the oven. Kids want to do the hands-on work—and they can! Of course, the amount of supervision required depends on the age of the child. And for kids who can't read yet, read the steps to them so they can follow along.

Most of the recipes yield small batches. This is by design. I limit the yield for sweets so there's just enough to share with a few with family and friends, avoiding leftover treats.

In the Your Restaurant Menu chapter, the recipes have slightly larger yields because the dishes are intended as contributions to family dinners for four. You can help the child increase the quantity if they want to serve a larger group. And the Your Kitchen Specials chapter is a collection of kid-friendly light meals and snacks to serve two or three children.

With these recipes, kids cook from scratch as much as possible. They're not fooled that real cooking is tossing together prepared foods. Here, kids mix their own doughs and stir their own batters and sauces. And they'll feel justly accomplished at the finish line.

Some recipes are for foods often only seen in packages. Yes, tackling a recipe is more work than buying it from the store, but what fun for kids to find out they can actually make their own crackers, tortilla chips, and bread!

Kids cook for the sheer joy of it. Set aside a leisurely amount of time for them to mix and measure unhurriedly.

Everyday Kitchen for Kids is the companion book to *Kids Kitchen*. The first book is a bestselling treasury of 100 classic treats and savoury recipes. While each book is a standalone, I hope children will have access to the full collection of recipes spanning both books. That's the reason I designed *Everyday Kitchen for Kids* with no duplications from *Kids Kitchen*.

This second book has a significantly expanded list of savoury recipes. And—as a new addition—it contains a selection of gluten-free recipes. Children who avoid gluten can now join in the kitchen fun. Some recipes just happen to be gluten-free, while others were created with that goal in mind. Kids who can eat gluten can still enjoy the gluten-free dishes.

When we see the look of amazement on a child's face as their creation comes out of the oven, we're reminded that cooking is actually a kind of magic. Let's enjoy every minute of it. Have fun in the kitchen!

Jennifer Low

Organising the Kitchen for Kids

PICK YOUR RECIPE!

Choose the recipe you want to make by taking a good, long look through the pages. Got something in mind? Check the baking, rising, or chilling times to make sure you have enough time to make the recipe. Take a look at the photo so you know what the recipe looks like when it's finished. It's helpful to keep it in mind as you create your dish!

READ BEFORE COOKING

You and your helpers should read this section on organising before getting started in the kitchen. Also read your selected recipe from beginning to end before you touch any ingredients. You don't have to read all of the Cook's Glossary (page 15) before you begin, but refer to it to clear up anything you don't understand in your recipe.

GET YOUR INGREDIENTS

Read the ingredients list closely. Make sure you have everything your recipe calls for. You don't want to be in the middle of a recipe only to discover you're missing an ingredient. Set out the ingredients in your work area. Notice that if you need soft butter, you need to take it out of the fridge the day before or several hours ahead so the butter can turn soft enough to scoop with a spoon.

Plan ahead when you want to cook so there's time to buy items you don't have. When buying small quantities of ingredients you don't use very often, your helper might want to check out bulk food stores, where you can get just the amount you need of speciality flours, decorating sprinkles, or baking chocolate instead of a full package.

GATHER YOUR SUPPLIES

The supplies you will need for each recipe are listed just before the ingredients. Most are common kitchen tools. Before you begin cooking, collect your supplies and put them near your work area.

In addition to the supplies listed, you might also want to keep handy a timer with an alarm. Your oven may also have a built-in timer. Ask for help in learning how to use it. Timers are important when cooking because it's easy to lose track of the minutes if you just rely on a watch or clock.

Other helpful tools are extra sets of measuring cups and spoons. Dry ingredients get stuck inside wet cups and spoons if you use the same one twice. If you have only one set of measuring cups and spoons, clean and dry them before re-using them.

Use baking spatulas made from heatproof materials.

USE THE RIGHT BOWLS

Don't use bowls that are too small to hold ingredients. Choose roomier ones with high sides that will keep ingredients from spilling out as you stir.

Many recipes call for "microwave-safe" bowls. These are usually made of glass or ceramics. Sometimes the bottom of a bowl will even say "microwave-safe". If you have any doubts whether you should use a bowl or not, ask your helper to take a look. Clear glass mixing bowls are especially good for microwaving because you can see the ingredients as they are heating.

BUTTER AND PAPER YOUR BAKING TINS

If your recipe needs a baking tin, you may need to put butter and parchment paper in it so your cake or bread comes out easily after baking. Prepare a baking tin by tracing out the bottom—round, rectangular, or square—onto a piece of parchment. Cut out a slightly smaller

shape than the tracing, then check that the cutout fits *flat* in the bottom of the tin and doesn't bend up the sides. Trim it until you get the size you need. Set the cutout aside. Using a pastry brush or scrunched-up piece of cling film, rub a blob of butter or margarine (or a dab of vegetable oil) onto the bottom and sides of the tin. Finally, press the cut-out parchment onto the buttered/oiled bottom. The tin is now ready for your dough or batter!

Baking sheets do not require buttering before putting parchment paper in the bottoms of them.

SOFTEN BUTTER AT ROOM TEMPERATURE

Unless butter is going to be melted, you will need *soft* butter. It needs to be soft enough to scoop with a spoon. It's best to leave it out of the fridge overnight—or for several hours—on your worktop at room temperature before using it.

MEASURE INGREDIENTS PROPERLY

When measuring ingredients, it's a good idea not to measure over your mixing bowl because a spill could ruin your recipe. Measure over an empty bowl instead.

Measuring dry ingredients

Measuring cups make measuring dry ingredients very easy for small children. Measuring cups come in assorted sizes in a set, usually from 1 cup (250 ml) to ⅓ cup (80 ml) and can be purchased for a few pounds. Although they're used to measure dry ingredients such as flour, sugar, icing sugar, unsweetened cocoa powder, or chocolate chips, they can also be used to measure things like soft butter.

To measure a dry ingredient, do *not* scoop your measuring cup into the ingredient bag or canister. This will pack in too much of the dry ingredient for your recipe. The correct method (except for brown sugar; see below) is to stir the ingredient in its bag or canister, then use a spoon to scoop the ingredient into the measuring cup until it overflows the rim. Scrape off the extra by pushing across the rim of the cup with a straight edge such as a dinner knife. Use this "spoon in, level" method for quantities of 4 tbsp or more. To measure 1 tbsp or less of a dry ingredient, just scoop the measuring spoon into the dry ingredient and level it off with the side of your finger or a dinner knife.

To measure brown sugar, press the soft sugar into the measuring cup until it is flat and level with the rim.

Measuring wet ingredients

Use a liquid measuring cup for wet ingredients such as water, milk, and juice. It is the cup with markings for assorted quantities on the side and a spout for pouring.

It can be tricky to measure spoonfuls of liquids such as extracts and vinegar without spilling. It's easier to pour a little of the ingredient into a small dish, then scoop your measuring spoon in to get the amount you need. If you have a new bottle of extract, a helper can pierce a hole in the foil top so the liquid will dribble out slowly and won't spill out when you pour.

To measure sticky ingredients like honey or molasses, rub the inside of the measuring spoon or cup with a dab of butter, margarine, or vegetable oil before filling it with your ingredient. The sticky stuff will slide out easily.

SET YOUR MICROWAVE OVEN TO THE RIGHT LEVELS

The microwave is often used to melt or warm small quantities of ingredients. When a recipe calls for 50% power, you would use level 5 if your microwave levels are 1 to 10 (if not, ask for help to figure out 50% power). When recipes call for the microwave to be on "high," it means level 10. Heating times may vary with different microwaves, so watch yours closely the first few times you use it and adjust times if necessary.

PUT YOUR OVEN RACK IN THE MIDDLE FOR BAKING

All baked recipes in this book use the middle rack of a regular oven. Before you preheat the oven, check that the rack is in the proper position.

Cook's Glossary

BAKING SHEET

Some recipes call for a "rimmed" baking sheet. If the type is not specified, then either rimmed or non-rimmed will work.

If you have only one baking sheet for a recipe that calls for two, you'll need to cool the sheet to room temperature before you put your next batch of dough onto it. Putting dough onto a warm baking sheet will not get the best results—for example, cookies will flatten more than they should.

If you do have two baking sheets, you should bake one at a time on the middle rack of the oven for even baking. If you put two sheets into the oven at once, the food on one sheet will brown more quickly than the other.

When lining a baking sheet with parchment paper, cut a piece of paper that fits the bottom of the sheet and lay it in place (no butter is needed). Cover as much of the baking sheet as you can.

BAKING SPATULA

Baking spatulas are great for stirring and scraping batter, yeast, and liquids out of bowls and cups. Use a dinner knife to scrape off ingredients that stick to the baking spatula while stirring.

Many baking spatulas are made of heatproof materials (see photo), which is especially important if you are stirring ingredients heated in the microwave.

BUTTER

How soft should "soft" butter be? You should be able to scoop it easily with a spoon. Leave butter out of the fridge overnight or several hours for best results.

When it comes to measuring butter, it is easier to cut off what you need than to fill measuring cups with butter. If you do use measuring cups, a small baking spatula is helpful for filling and removing soft butter.

If unsalted butter is not specified, then either salted or unsalted can be used.

All recipes were developed with butter. Margarine can be substituted, but results may vary.

CHILL

Put in the refrigerator to cool.

COCOA POWDER

This is unsweetened cocoa powder, not a cocoa mix that also contains sugar.

CORNFLOUR

Cornflour is not the same as ordinary flour.

CREAM CHEESE

How soft should "soft" cream cheese be? It should be soft enough that you can easily press a spoon into it.

CREAM INGREDIENTS

When you "cream" ingredients, there's actually no cream involved. To cream means to use the back of a wooden spoon to mash together ingredients, often butter and sugar, until they are blended.

DINNER KNIFE

This is an ordinary knife you'd use to eat with at the dinner table. It is just sharp enough to cut soft things—like dough—but not sharp enough to hurt you.

In addition to cutting, a dinner knife is useful for scraping sticky ingredients off baking spatulas or wooden spoons when stirring.

DRINKING CUP

An ordinary cup—not too big—that you might normally drink from. This kind of cup is useful for holding foaming yeast.

EGGS

This book's recipes work with any size of chicken eggs.

Some recipes require separating eggs, which means the yolks and whites are separated. To do this, it's easiest to use an egg separator—it looks like a big spoon with slots in it. Some types of separators clip to bowl rims while others are balanced across the top of a bowl. Crack an egg and drop the insides into the egg separator. The yolk will stay in the separator while the egg white drains out into the bowl underneath.

If you do not have an egg separator, you can carefully crack an egg in half over a bowl and pour the egg from one half of the shell to the other half until the egg white drips into the bowl, leaving the yolk in the shell. You could also ask a helper for a hand with this step. If bits of yolk or shell get into the egg white, carefully scoop them out with the edge of the split eggshell or with a small spoon.

FOLD

This is a different meaning than to fold paper. With food, "fold" means to gently mix together fluffy ingredients while keeping them fluffy. To do this, use a baking spatula to slice big circles under and over the ingredients in a bowl, turning them over and over until they are mixed.

FROSTING CAKES

See "Tips on Frosting Cakes," page 125, for pointers on how to frost a cake without smearing the plate and how to avoid cake crumbs in the frosting.

GARLIC POWDER AND GARLIC SALT

These are not the same thing. Garlic powder is only garlic flavour, not saltiness. It is often sold as a powder and may have clumps in it that need to be mashed out before using. Garlic salt is garlicky and salty. It usually has a grainy texture similar to salt.

GET HELP

When you see the words "Get help" or "Ask a helper," it means that step could be tricky and should be done by an adult, like pulling hot stuff out of the oven. Since you are the boss of your recipe, there are not too many times where you're asked to get help, but when you see this instruction be sure to follow it.

GLUTEN-FREE

These recipes do not call for gluten-rich ingredients such as wheat flour or breadcrumbs (or they have a gluten-free option). Gluten-free plain flour contains assorted flours. Only recipes that call for less than 125ml (½ cup) of plain flour are marked [GF]. Results may vary if you substitute gluten-free plain flour in recipes that call for more than 125 ml (½ cup) of plain flour.

You must check the label to find out if packaged ingredients such as soy sauce contain gluten. Recipes calling for oats are not marked [GF]. However, some kinds of oats can be eaten on gluten-free diets, and recipes calling for oats can be made gluten-free for you if you use a reliable oat product. And, note that gluten-free foods are fine to eat even if you can eat gluten!

GRADUALLY

To add an ingredient "gradually" means to add it in three or four portions to the other ingredients, mixing after each addition.

MASA HARINA

Also called "instant corn masa mix," masa harina is a kind of flour made from corn that is sold in many supermarkets and speciality food stores. It is not the same as cornflour or cornmeal.

MICROWAVE

To heat something in the microwave "at 50% power" means that the power should be on level 5 if your microwave levels are 1 to 10 (if not, ask for help to figure out 50% power). To get to 5, push on the power button repeatedly. The setting moves down one level each time you press, counting down from 10. Ask someone for help if you need it. When recipes call for the microwave to be on "high," it means level 10.

£2-COIN RULE

When rolling dough to 2 mm thick, set a £2 coin nearby to compare to your dough. A £2 coin is about the right thickness. If you don't have a £2, ask a helper to find another coin that is about 2 mm thick and keep it handy for your baking.

ONION POWDER AND ONION SALT

These are not the same thing. Onion powder is not salty, only oniony. Onion salt has both an onion taste and saltiness.

ORDINARY TEASPOON

Some recipes call for an ordinary teaspoon for scooping and stirring. This is any spoon you would usually use to stir a drink. The size of the spoon's bowl does not matter in this instance.

OVEN (REGULAR)

All baked recipes in this book should use the middle rack of the regular (not microwave) oven. This means the rack is set halfway between the top and bottom of the oven.

PARCHMENT PAPER

This is a kind of non-stick paper for lining baking sheets and tins so foods don't stick to them. The paper is sold in rolls or sheets in supermarkets. It is available in white or brown. It is sometimes called baking paper or silicone paper. It is *not* wax paper. If heated, the wax on wax paper melts and makes a mess.

PIZZA WHEEL

A pizza wheel can be used as a safe cutting tool for kids. Sharpness varies depending on the metal or plastic wheels. Do not put hands in the path of the wheel.

POTATO STARCH

Same as potato flour.

PRE-GRATED CHEESE

When a recipe calls for pre-grated cheese, this refers to either store-bought grated cheese or cheese that has been grated by a helper. Kids are asked to avoid using graters, since their multiple blades are sharp!

RICE FLOUR

Rice flour is often used in gluten-free recipes and is available in white or brown rice varieties. White rice flour is also available in "regular" or "glutinous" types. Though "glutinous" sounds like "gluten," they're not the same things at all. Glutinous white rice flour does not contain gluten; it just means that it's made from sticky rice. Even more confusing, glutinous rice flour is also sometimes labelled "sweet rice flour" even though it has no sweet taste and contains no sugar or sweetener.

SALT

What is a pinch of salt? Squeeze as much salt as you can between your thumb and pointer finger. That's a pinch. A sprinkle of salt from a shaker will also do.

SIEVE

A fine mesh sieve can be used to sift dry ingredients.

SOFT BUTTER

See Organising the Kitchen for Kids: Soften Butter at Room Temperature, page 13.

SPOON IN, LEVEL

"Spoon in, level" is a reminder *not* to scoop your measuring cup into the ingredient to fill it. When measuring ¼ cups (or more) of dry ingredients, such as flour, *spoon* the ingredient into your measuring cup into an overflowing mound, then use a straight edge—like a dinner knife—to scrape across the top of the cup so the ingredient is flat and *level* with the rim.

TAPIOCA STARCH

Same as tapioca flour.

TWO-STACKED-POUND-COINS RULE

The height of a stack of two £1 coins is almost equal to 5 mm and just a little under 6 mm. When you're rolling cookie and pastry doughs to that thickness, it's easier to stack two coins near your work board and compare their height to your dough than it is to read the tiny markings on a ruler.

UNSWEETENED COCOA POWDER

See cocoa powder.

WHIPPED CREAM

This is fluffy cream that has *already* been whipped. When a recipe calls for "whipped cream," the amount listed is for the whipped volume. You can also substitute whipped topping if you wish.

WHIPPING CREAM

This is the liquid cream containing 35% milk fat. When a recipe calls for "whipping cream," the quantity listed is for the liquid volume.

WHISK

Whisks are not used for whipping ingredients in this book; they are used for stirring. A stiff "balloon" whisk (long, oval wire loops) works best. Check that the handle is not too long or awkward to use.

YEAST

Quick-rise instant yeast is the type used in this book. It is in dry granules and commonly sold in packets or jars.

The yeast needs to grow in very warm water before you use it. Run tap water until it is very warm but still a comfortable temperature to touch. If it's too cool, yeast won't grow. If it's too hot, it will kill the yeast. Place yeast and sugar into a bowl or cup, add the very warm water, and cover with cling film to keep the mixture warm so it will turn foamy. The sugar helps the yeast grow. Use the entire foamy yeast mixture in your recipe—that is, *all the liquid and the foam*.

Yeast dough likes a warm place to rise. Where's best? Place the bowl next to or on top of a warm oven—but not inside it! If you're using a plastic bowl, be sure the top of the oven isn't too hot. Metal mixing bowls work well for rising dough since they pick up heat easily and you don't need to worry about the temperature of your oven top.

If neither your oven nor kitchen is warm, put your bowl of foaming yeast in the oven or microwave (not turned on!), set a bowl of very warm water next to it (get help with this!), and close the oven door for ten minutes.

Some of the most scrumptious recipes are made with yeast. It's really worth waiting for the dough to rise because you'll be able to make recipes that look and taste like they came from a fancy bakery!

your restaurant menu

Cook a delicious main or side
dish to help with the family meal!

French Toast in a Pan

[breakfast]

SUPPLIES

pastry brush or cling film, 20 cm square glass baking dish, kitchen scissors, bowls, measuring cups, measuring spoons, whisk, wooden spoon

INGREDIENTS

soft butter for baking dish

4 slices whole wheat or white bread

6 eggs

330 ml milk

⅛ tsp vanilla extract

pinch of salt

GLAZE

1 tbsp unsalted butter

2 tbsp packed brown sugar

4 tbsp maple syrup

maple syrup to serve

fresh fruit such as berries, bananas, or
   peaches to serve

You can cook Good Morning Bacon! (page 24) or a Batch o' Brekkie Sausages (page 26) at the same time as this recipe for breakfast.

1. Use a pastry brush or scrunched-up piece of cling film to butter the bottom and sides of the baking dish.

2. Use kitchen scissors to cut each slice of bread into four triangles by cutting each slice in half diagonally, then cutting each half slice in half. Leave crusts on. Overlap the triangles in two rows inside the baking dish. Put the crust sides on the bottom. Make sure the bread covers as much of the bottom of the dish as possible (don't worry about small gaps). Set aside.

3. In a large bowl, whisk together the eggs, milk, vanilla, and salt until well mixed. Pour over the bread. Use the back of a wooden spoon to press down gently on the bread. Let stand for 10 minutes. Don't worry if the egg mixture isn't soaked in completely at this point.

4. Meanwhile, preheat the oven to 180°C/160°C fan/gas 4.

5. To make the glaze, place the 1 tbsp of butter in a microwave-safe bowl and heat in the microwave at 50% power until melted (about 30 seconds). Mix in the brown sugar and maple syrup.

6. After the bread's 10-minute soak, use the back of the wooden spoon again to press down gently on it so the bread sops up even more of the egg mixture.

7. Drizzle the glaze overtop.

8. Bake on the middle rack of the oven for 35 to 40 minutes, uncovered, until the bread puffs up (it settles back down after it comes out of the oven) and turns lightly golden. Cool until warm before slicing and serving with more maple syrup and fresh fruit.

Serves 4 to 6.

FRENCH TOAST IN A PAN

Good Morning Bacon!

[*breakfast*] [GF]

SUPPLIES

large rimmed baking sheet, parchment paper, 3 paper towels, heatproof tongs, large plate

INGREDIENTS

4 to 12 slices bacon (find out how many strips your family wants to eat—for example, 1, 2, or 3 slices per person—and add them up)

This recipe makes up to 12 slices of bacon, but the quantity can be sized up or down depending on how many people you are making breakfast for. You can cook the bacon at the same time as the French Toast in a Pan (page 22).

1. Preheat the oven to 180°C/160°C fan/gas 4.

2. Line a rimmed baking sheet with parchment paper.

3. Lay the strips of bacon on the parchment. Keep the slices a little apart.

4. If you are cooking the bacon at the same time as the French Toast in a Pan, place the baking sheet with the bacon on the top rack of the oven and the French Toast pan on the middle rack. If you're just cooking the bacon, it's okay to use the middle rack.

5. Cook in the oven for 15 to 30 minutes. Check the bacon carefully in the last few minutes so you can get help removing it from the oven when it is at the crispiness you like.

6. Place two paper towels on a plate. Let the bacon cool a little before you use tongs to pick up the bacon (let grease drip back onto the baking sheet) and place it on the paper towels. Gently press another paper towel onto the bacon to soak up remaining grease.

Makes 4 to 12 slices of Good Morning Bacon!

BATCH O' BREKKIE SAUSAGES (PAGE 26) AND
GOOD MORNING BACON!

Batch o' Brekkie Sausages

[breakfast] [GF]

SUPPLIES

large rimmed baking sheet, parchment paper, 3 paper towels, heatproof tongs, large plate

INGREDIENTS

4 to 12 breakfast sausages (find out how many sausages your family wants to eat—1, 2, or 3 per person—and add them up)

PICTURED ON PAGE 25

Cook these on their own or in the same oven as the French Toast in a Pan (page 22). The sausages come out of the oven a little before the French Toast is done.

(1) Preheat the oven to 180°C/160°C fan/gas 4.

(2) Line a rimmed baking sheet with parchment paper.

(3) Lay the sausages on the parchment, keeping the sausages from touching each other.

(4) If you are cooking the sausages at the same time as the French Toast in a Pan, place the baking sheet with the sausages on the top rack of the oven and the French Toast pan on the middle rack. If you're just cooking the sausages, it's okay to use the middle rack.

(5) Cook in the oven for 15 to 30 minutes, or until the sausages are browned on top.

(6) Place two paper towels on a plate. Let the sausages cool a little before you use tongs to pick them up and place them onto the paper towels. Gently press another paper towel on top to soak up remaining grease.

Makes 4 to 12 Brekkie Sausages.

Cashew Couscous (Bless You!)

[side dish]

SUPPLIES

1.5 litre glass or ceramic baking dish, baking spatula or wooden spoon, measuring cups, measuring spoons, kitchen scissors, microwave-safe measuring cup or bowl, foil (or lid of baking dish), fork

INGREDIENTS

250 ml (1 cup) couscous

1 tsp olive oil

1 spring onion

5 tbsp roasted cashew pieces

2 tbsp sultana raisins

½ tsp dried parsley

½ tsp finely chopped garlic (from jar)

¼ tsp ground cumin

pinch of salt

500 ml water

1 tbsp butter

PICTURED ON PAGE 57

Couscous is actually tiny pieces of pasta almost as small as grains of sand. Each forkful of this recipe is deliciously different!

1. Preheat the oven to 180°C/160°C fan/gas 4.

2. In the baking dish and using a baking spatula or wooden spoon, mix the couscous and olive oil until the couscous is well coated.

3. Use kitchen scissors to snip the spring onion in little pieces about the size of your fingernail into the couscous (throw away or compost the root).

4. Stir in the cashew pieces, raisins, parsley, garlic, cumin, and salt.

5. Place the water in a microwave-safe measuring cup or bowl, and heat in the microwave on high for 1 minute. Remove the water from the microwave and stir into the couscous mixture.

6. Cover the baking dish tightly with a lid or foil. Get help putting the dish on the middle rack of the oven. Bake for 30 minutes.

7. Get help removing the couscous from the oven and uncovering. Cool until the dish is just warm.

8. Add the butter to the couscous and stir with a fork until fluffy.

Makes 750 ml.

Roasted Tomato and Bocconcini Salad [*side dish*] [GF]

SUPPLIES

knife (for helper), measuring cup, measuring spoons, rimmed baking sheet, parchment paper, bowl, baking spatula, kitchen scissors

INGREDIENTS

500 to 750 ml (2 to 3 cups) cherry tomatoes

2 tbsp olive oil

1 tbsp balsamic vinegar

1 tsp runny honey

3 golf ball–sized or 6 olive-sized balls bocconcini cheese

fresh basil leaves

pinch of each salt and pepper

Roasting tomatoes this way makes them taste even sweeter! Bocconcini is a round white cheese that soaks up flavours.

1. Preheat the oven to 200°C/180°C fan/gas 6.

2. Get help cutting the cherry tomatoes in half lengthwise.

3. Line a baking sheet with parchment paper.

4. In a big bowl and using a baking spatula, mix the olive oil, balsamic vinegar, and honey (rub some olive oil in the teaspoon before filling it with honey so it slides out easily). Add the tomato halves and stir gently with the baking spatula to coat them.

5. Scoop the tomatoes onto the parchment paper, keeping the extra liquid in the bowl to use later.

6. Now you have to use your eagle eyes and turn over every tomato half so that the cut sides are facing up. They roast better when the wet insides of the tomato halves are face-up.

7. Roast tomatoes on the middle rack of the oven for 10 to 15 minutes, or until they have shrunken in size a little but are not mushy looking.

8. Meanwhile, use kitchen scissors to cut the bocconcini cheese into bite-sized pieces. Put them into the bowl of leftover liquid from the tomatoes. Use the scissors to snip the basil leaves into little pieces into the bowl. Also add the salt and pepper.

9. After the tomatoes are cooked, let them cool to room temperature then add them to the bowl with the cheese and basil. Stir gently with a baking spatula to coat everything.

Makes 4 servings.

ROASTED TOMATO AND

BOCCONCINI SALAD

FEAST RICE

Feast Rice

[side dish] [GF]

SUPPLIES

microwave-safe 1.5 litre glass or ceramic baking dish, measuring cups, measuring spoons, baking spatula or wooden spoon, ordinary teaspoon, foil (or lid of baking dish), bowl, fork, kitchen scissors, oven mitts

INGREDIENTS

375 ml chicken or vegetable broth

2 tbsp oyster sauce

185 ml (¾ cup) long-grain white rice

1 tbsp vegetable oil

½ tsp finely chopped garlic (from jar)

250 ml (1 cup) frozen mixed peas and diced carrots (or ask a helper to dice fresh carrot and celery)

¼ tsp sesame oil

2 eggs

1 tbsp milk

pinch of salt

1 spring onion

If you like Chinese fried rice, this recipe—often served at big parties or feasts—lets you try out cool Asian ingredients to make your own version without any frying.

1. Preheat the oven to 190°C/170°C fan/gas 5.

2. In the baking dish and using a baking spatula or wooden spoon, mix the broth and oyster sauce. Heat in the microwave on high for 1 minute.

3. Remove the dish from the microwave. Using an ordinary teaspoon, stir in the rice, vegetable oil, garlic, peas and carrots, and sesame oil.

4. Spread out the rice evenly in the baking dish, then cover tightly with a lid or foil. Get help putting the dish in the oven. Bake on the middle rack of the oven for 30 minutes.

5. In the meantime, place the eggs, milk, and salt in a bowl and beat with a fork.

6. After the rice has baked 30 minutes, get help removing the lid or foil. Pour the egg mixture onto the middle of the rice. Do not stir. Cover the dish again and bake for another 10 to 15 minutes, until you can't see any more liquid (If you are using a glass dish, you can see if there's liquid bubbling around the sides of the rice. If you can't see through your baking dish, ask a helper to help you check if the liquid is gone.)

7. Get help removing the dish from the oven and taking off the cover. Use kitchen scissors to snip the green onion into small pieces about the size of your smallest fingernail onto the rice. Throw away or compost the roots. Wear oven mitts, or get help, to stir the rice with a fork to fluff. Eat while warm.

Makes 1 litre (4 cups).

Simple Rice and Peas

[side dish] [GF]

SUPPLIES

measuring cups, sieve, bowl, microwave-safe 1.5 litre glass or ceramic baking dish, measuring spoon, ordinary teaspoon, foil (or lid of baking dish), oven mitts, fork

INGREDIENTS

250 ml (1 cup) long-grain white rice

500 ml chicken or vegetable broth

2 tbsp butter

125 ml (½ cup) frozen peas

PICTURED ON PAGE 49

If your family is having chicken or pork chops for dinner, this would be a great side dish.

1. Preheat the oven to 190°C/170°C fan/gas 5.

2. Put the rice in the sieve and run it under cold tap water to rinse. Place the sieve of rice over a bowl to drain.

3. Place the broth and butter in the baking dish, then heat in the microwave on high for 1 minute to warm the broth and melt the butter. Take the dish out of the microwave and mix in the rice and peas. Spread out the mixture evenly in the dish.

4. Cover the baking dish tightly with a lid or foil. Bake on the middle rack of the oven for 40 minutes.

5. Get help removing the dish from the oven and taking off the cover. Wear oven mitts, or get help, to stir the rice with a fork to fluff.

Makes 625 ml.

Cinnamon Baby Carrots

[*side dish*] [GF]

These are a sweet addition to the dinner plate. Ask your family if these carrots will go with the meal they're making.

SUPPLIES

1.5 litre glass or ceramic baking dish, baking spatula or wooden spoon, measuring cups, measuring spoons, foil

INGREDIENTS

4 tbsp water

1 tbsp olive oil

2 tbsp runny honey

¼ tsp dried parsley

⅛ tsp chilli powder

⅛ tsp ground cinnamon

pinch of pepper

500 ml (2 cups) baby carrots

squeeze of fresh lemon juice, if
  you wish

1 Preheat the oven to 190°C/170°C fan/gas 5.

2 In the baking dish and using a baking spatula or wooden spoon, mix the water, olive oil, honey, parsley, chilli powder, cinnamon, and pepper. Stir in the carrots to coat with the spices.

3 Cover the baking dish tightly with a lid or foil. Bake on the middle rack of the oven for 25 to 30 minutes, or until the carrots are tender.

4 Get help removing the dish from the oven. Squeeze a few drops of lemon juice on top before serving, if you like.

Makes 4 servings.

BAKER'S DOZEN CHIVE BISCUITS

Baker's Dozen Chive Biscuits

[side dish]

SUPPLIES

baking sheet, parchment paper, bowls, baking spatula, measuring cups, measuring spoons, kitchen scissors, whisk, dinner knife, work board, 5 cm round cookie cutter

INGREDIENTS

375 ml (1½ cups) plain flour (spoon in, level; see page 19)

1½ tsp white sugar

2 tsp baking powder

¼ tsp salt

8 to 10 stalks chives

5 tbsp mayonnaise

5 tbsp milk

Eat these crunchy-on-top, soft little bread biscuits with a dab of butter while warm, or use them to sop up gravies and sauces.

1. Preheat the oven to 180°C/160°C fan/gas 4.

2. Line a baking sheet with parchment paper. Then cut a second sheet about half the size.

3. In a large bowl and using a baking spatula, mix together the flour, sugar, baking powder, and salt. Use kitchen scissors to cut the chives into little pieces the size of grains of rice into another bowl (hold the stalks together in a bunch to cut a few stalks at a time). Measure out 2 tbsp of chives and stir them into the flour mixture. Set aside.

4. In another bowl, whisk the mayonnaise and milk until smooth. Use the baking spatula to scrape the mixture into the bowl of dry ingredients, then stir them together. Scrape the spatula with a dinner knife to make sure everything is well blended. When the dough gets too stiff to stir, use your hands—keeping the dough inside the bowl—to roll and pat the rest of the dry ingredients into the dough.

5. Put the dough on the smaller piece of parchment. Pat the dough into a 1 cm thick slab. Cut out rounds with the cookie cutter. Make sure your cutouts are touching to get the most biscuits from the dough.

6. Place the cutouts on the parchment-lined baking sheet 2.5 cm apart. Squeeze together the scrap dough, pat down to 1 cm again and re-cut with the cookie cutter. You should have enough dough to make 13 biscuits in total, but don't worry if you get one less or more.

7. Place the remaining cutouts on the parchment paper. Bake for 25 minutes, or until the bottoms of the biscuits are golden. Get help checking the bottoms since the baking sheet is hot. Eat while warm.

Makes 13 biscuits—a baker's dozen!

Smashed Mini Potatoes

[side dish] [GF]

SUPPLIES

glass or ceramic baking dish just large enough to hold potatoes in one layer, measuring cups, measuring spoons, foil (or lid of baking dish), fork, bowl, coffee mug or rolling pin, pastry brush, ordinary teaspoon

INGREDIENTS

20 to 24 mini potatoes (each up to 4 cm wide/700 g in total)

4 tbsp water

4 tbsp butter

⅛ tsp each paprika, salt and pepper

2 tbsp pre-grated Parmesan cheese

Browned at the edges, tender and creamy in the middle: these are simply smashing at supper!

1. Preheat the oven to 200°C/180°C fan/gas 6.

2. Wash dirt off the potatoes. You don't have to peel them. Spread the potatoes in a single layer in the baking dish. Pour in the water. Set aside.

3. Place the butter in a microwave-safe bowl and heat at 50% power until melted (about 1 minute). Drizzle 1 tbsp of the melted butter over the potatoes. Set the rest of the melted butter aside.

4. Cover the dish of potatoes tightly with a lid or foil.

5. Bake on the middle rack of the oven for 45 minutes.

6. Get help taking the dish out of the oven and removing the lid or foil (keep the oven on). The potatoes should be soft enough to pierce easily with a fork; if they are not tender enough, cover them again and bake a few more minutes. Cool the potatoes for about 10 minutes so they're easier to handle.

7. Use the bottom of a coffee mug or a rolling pin to press down on the potatoes. You need to flatten the potatoes and split them open.

8. Go back to the dish of melted butter. It's okay if it has firmed up a bit; the butter will still be soft. Mix in the paprika, salt, and pepper. Use a pastry brush to dab the tops of the potatoes with the mixture. Using an ordinary teaspoon, sprinkle the potatoes with Parmesan cheese by holding spoonfuls of the Parmesan over the potatoes while you gently tap the handle to make the cheese fall evenly.

9. Put the dish of potatoes back in the oven to bake, uncovered, another 15 minutes. When serving, turn the potatoes over to show their golden side.

Makes 20 to 24 Smashed Mini Potatoes.

SMASHED MINI POTATOES

Upside-Down Baked Potatoes

[*side dish*] [GF]

SUPPLIES

bowl, measuring cup, measuring spoons, rimmed baking sheet, parchment paper, tea towel, knife (for helper), ordinary teaspoon, pastry brush, fork

INGREDIENTS

6 tbsp pre-grated Parmesan cheese

¼ tsp chilli powder

pinch of salt

2 tbsp vegetable oil

4 russet potatoes (the brown oval ones for baking)

These are so good, you don't need butter or sour cream on them. Ask a helper to cut the potatoes, then you can get them ready for baking.

1. Preheat the oven to 190°C/170°C fan/gas 5.

2. In a large bowl, mix the Parmesan cheese, chilli powder, and salt. Set aside.

3. Line a baking sheet with parchment paper. Drizzle the vegetable oil onto the parchment. Set aside.

4. Wash any dirt off the skin of the potatoes under cold tap water. Pat potatoes dry with a clean tea towel. Ask a helper to cut each potato in half lengthwise.

5. Place the potato halves—cut side down—on the oiled parchment paper. Swirl the halves on the oil to coat the cut sides completely.

6. Now you'll coat the cut side of each potato half with the cheese mixture. To do this, hold each potato half over the bowl of cheese mixture—cut side face up. Use an ordinary teaspoon to scoop some of the mixture and shake a thin layer over the cut side of the potato. Shake right over the edges to cover the entire cut side. Let the extra cheese fall back into the bowl.

7. Turn the potato half back over so the cheese-coated side is facing down, and put it on the parchment paper. Don't move the potato after it's on the parchment or the cheese might rub off. Coat all eight potato halves and place them on the parchment.

8. Dip a pastry brush into the oil on the parchment paper and lightly brush the potato skins. To prevent the potatoes from sliding as you brush, hold them down with your fingers.

9. Bake on the middle rack of the oven for 25 to 30 minutes, or until the potatoes are soft enough to be pierced with a fork.

10. Get help removing the baking sheet from the oven and turning the potatoes over to serve them. They will have a golden crust on the cheese side.

Makes 8 Upside-Down Baked Potatoes.

UPSIDE-DOWN BAKED POTATOES

Buttered Green Beans

[side dish] [GF]

SUPPLIES

colander, kitchen scissors, 1.5 litre glass or ceramic baking dish, measuring cups, foil, measuring spoons, baking spatula or wooden spoon

INGREDIENTS

4 big handfuls green beans

5 tbsp water

1 tsp butter

pinch of each salt and pepper

PICTURED ON PAGE 58

Steam fresh green beans in the oven. When you cook veggies yourself, they taste better!

1. Preheat the oven to 190°C/170°C fan/gas 5.

2. Before you cook the green beans, you need to wash and trim them. To do that, put them in a colander and run under cold water. Drain. To trim, use kitchen scissors to snip off the stems from the beans (throw the stems away), then snip each bean in half, crosswise, so you end up with two shorter sections.

3. Put the beans into the baking dish. Add the water. Cover the baking dish tightly with a lid or foil.

4. Bake on the middle rack of the oven for 25 to 30 minutes, or until the beans are tender.

5. Get help removing the dish from the oven. With a baking spatula or wooden spoon, stir in the butter, salt, and pepper.

Makes 4 servings.

Parmesan Risotto

[side dish] [GF]

SUPPLIES

measuring spoons, microwave-safe
1.5 litre glass or ceramic baking dish,
baking spatula or wooden spoon,
measuring cups

INGREDIENTS

1 tbsp butter

250 ml (1 cup) Arborio rice

1 tbsp basil pesto

2 tsp dried onion flakes

pinch of nutmeg

pinch of pepper

500 ml vegetable or chicken broth

250 ml milk

250 ml water

1 bay leaf

5 tbsp pre-grated Parmesan cheese

PICTURED ON PAGE 54

Risotto is a recipe for a kind of soft rice. This one has a golden crust of cheese.

1. Preheat the oven to 180°C/160°C fan/gas 4.

2. Put the butter into the baking dish and heat in the microwave at 50% power until melted (about 30 seconds). Use a baking spatula or wooden spoon to stir in the Arborio rice, basil pesto, onion flakes, nutmeg, and pepper. Mix well.

3. Add the vegetable or chicken broth, milk, water, and bay leaf to the baking dish. Heat in the microwave at 50% power for 1½ minutes. Get help removing the dish from the microwave. The rice will be covered by the liquids.

4. Sprinkle the Parmesan cheese on the liquid. Do not stir. Get help putting the baking dish on the middle rack of the oven. Bake (uncovered) for 35 to 40 minutes, or until the top is lightly golden.

Makes 750 ml.

RICE, ORZO, AND SPLIT PEA TRIO

Rice, Orzo, and Split Pea Trio

[side dish]

SUPPLIES

measuring cups, measuring spoons, microwave-safe 1.5 litre glass or ceramic baking dish, wooden spoon, foil (or lid of baking dish), ordinary teaspoon, oven mitts, fork

INGREDIENTS

750 ml vegetable or chicken broth

1 tbsp butter

5 tbsp long-grain white rice

5 tbsp orzo pasta (looks like big pieces of rice)

5 tbsp dried yellow split peas

1 bay leaf

1 whole clove

1 tbsp dried onion flakes

1 tsp dried parsley

pinch each of nutmeg, salt, and pepper

When you can't decide between rice or pasta— eat both! Funny thing is, orzo is a small pasta that looks almost like rice. And a whole clove is a spice that looks like a little brown flower.

1. Preheat the oven to 190°C/170°C fan/gas 5.

2. Pour the broth and butter into the baking dish. Heat in the microwave on high for 1 minute to warm the broth and melt the butter. Get help removing the dish from the microwave.

3. Using a wooden spoon, stir in the rice, orzo, split peas, bay leaf, whole clove, onion flakes, parsley, nutmeg, salt, and pepper. Spread out the rice mixture evenly.

4. Cover the baking dish with a lid or foil, and get help putting it in the oven. Bake for 45 minutes until the liquid is almost all gone.

5. Get help removing the dish from the oven and uncovering. Cool slightly, then wear oven mitts, or get help, to stir the mixture with a fork to fluff. Cover again for 3 minutes (do not put in the oven again) to let the rest of the broth absorb into the rice, pasta, and peas before eating.

Makes 750 ml.

Unfried Picnic Chicken Drumsticks

[*main*] [GF]

SUPPLIES

measuring cups; 3 wide, shallow bowls; measuring spoons; whisk; ordinary teaspoon; rimmed baking sheet; parchment paper; pastry brush or cling film

INGREDIENTS

FLOUR COATING

125 ml (½ cup) plain flour (regular or gluten-free) (spoon in, level; see page 19)

YOGURT COATING

1 egg

5 tbsp milk

5 tbsp plain yogurt

1 tbsp vegetable oil

SPICE CRUST

125 ml (½ cup) plain flour (regular or gluten-free) (spoon in, level)

125 ml (½ cup) instant skim milk powder

1 tsp celery salt

1 tsp paprika

½ tsp dry mustard

½ tsp garlic salt

½ tsp white sugar

¼ tsp chilli powder

⅛ tsp ground nutmeg

2 tbsp vegetable oil

8 to 10 skinless chicken drumsticks

So scrumptious! Tastes like the best fried chicken, but the golden crust is skinless and baked. This looks like a long list of spices, but they might already be in your cupboard. Don't skip any!

1   Preheat the oven to 180°C/160°C fan/gas 4.

2   Now you will set up a chicken-coating assembly line. First, place the flour coating into a wide shallow bowl. Next to that, in another shallow bowl, whisk together the yogurt coating ingredients until smooth. Next to that, in a third shallow bowl, use an ordinary teaspoon to mix together the spice crust ingredients (don't add the vegetable oil into the bowl). These three bowls should now be in a row on your counter.

3   Place the baking sheet next to the spice crust bowl. Line it with parchment paper and drizzle the vegetable oil on it. Rub the oil over the parchment with either a pastry brush or a scrunched-up piece of cling film.

4   Now you're ready to coat the chicken. Pick up a chicken drumstick and roll it in the flour to coat it completely. Next, roll the floured chicken in the yogurt coating. Then hold the drumstick by the bone end and roll it in the spice crust. Your hands will get messy, but that's okay. Place the drumstick onto the baking sheet. Coat all the drumsticks with the same steps.

5   Wash and dry your hands. Using the ordinary teaspoon you used to mix your spice crust ingredients, sprinkle any remaining spice crust mixture onto the drumsticks. The more spice crust you stick onto the chicken, the tastier it will be. Throw away the leftover stuff in the bowls.

6   Bake the chicken for 40 minutes. Get help after 20 minutes of baking to turn the chicken over. Continue baking until the drumsticks are golden and cooked through.

Makes 8 to 10 Unfried Picnic Chicken Drumsticks.

UNFRIED PICNIC CHICKEN DRUMSTICKS

BEEF STEW OOH-LA-LA

Beef Stew Ooh-La-La

[main] [GF]

SUPPLIES

rimmed baking sheet, parchment paper, kitchen scissors, measuring cups, measuring spoons, bowl, 23 × 33 cm glass or ceramic baking dish, wooden spoon

INGREDIENTS

2 slices bacon

125 ml (½ cup) plain flour (regular or gluten-free) (spoon in, level; see page 19)

½ tsp paprika

¼ tsp salt

⅛ tsp pepper

750 g cubed stewing beef

500 ml beef broth

185 ml tomato sauce

125 ml unsweetened apple juice

1 bay leaf

1 tbsp dried onion flakes

1 tsp finely chopped garlic (from jar)

1 tsp dried parsley

1 tsp dried thyme

couple handfuls baby carrots

couple handfuls pre-sliced mushrooms

This recipe is like a fancy French dish called *boeuf bourguignon.* Luckily, you don't have to say it to cook it.

1. Preheat the oven to 190°C/170°C fan/gas 5.

2. Line a baking sheet with parchment paper.

3. Use kitchen scissors to cut the slices of bacon into ½-inch (1 cm) pieces. Spread them out on the lined baking sheet and set aside, then wash your hands.

4. In a large bowl, mix the flour, paprika, salt, and pepper. Add the cubed beef. Use your hands to roll all sides of the meat in the flour mixture.

5. Put the meat on top of the pieces of bacon, leaving the extra flour mixture in the bowl, then wash your hands. Throw away the stuff in the bowl. Bake for 15 minutes. Get help turning the pieces of meat over, then bake for another 10 or 15 minutes, or until the meat is lightly browned. Remove the baking sheet from the oven and set aside, but leave the oven on.

6. In the baking dish and using the wooden spoon, mix the beef broth, tomato sauce, apple juice, bay leaf, onion flakes, garlic, parsley, and thyme. Add the carrots and mushrooms, then add the beef and bacon.

7. Get help putting the dish into the oven. Bake, uncovered, for about 1 hour, or until the meat is browned on top and the sauce is thickened and bubbly.

Makes 4 servings.

Coconut-Curry Kookoo Chicken

[*main*] [GF]

SUPPLIES

bowl, whisk, measuring cups,
measuring spoons, can opener,
23 × 33 cm glass or ceramic
baking dish

INGREDIENTS

125 ml chicken broth

1 tbsp plain flour (regular or
   gluten-free)

1 can (400 g) unsweetened coconut
   milk

5 tbsp tomato sauce

1 tbsp dried onion flakes

1 tbsp vegetable oil

1 tsp white sugar

1 tsp curry powder

1 tsp finely chopped garlic (from jar)

½ tsp ground cumin

¼ tsp salt

8 to 10 skinless chicken drumsticks

5 tbsp sweetened or unsweetened
   shredded coconut

If your family likes Indian food, try this dish that makes its own curry sauce. Ask your family to make rice to serve with this so you can spoon the sauce over it.

1. Preheat the oven to 190°C/170°C fan/gas 5.

2. In a bowl, whisk the chicken broth and flour until smooth. Then whisk in the coconut milk, tomato sauce, onion flakes, vegetable oil, sugar, curry powder, garlic, cumin, and salt. Pour this sauce into the baking dish.

3. Put the chicken drumsticks into the sauce. Roll them around to coat.

4. Get help putting the baking dish into the oven. Bake for 30 minutes. Get help turning the drumsticks over in the sauce, then bake for another 15 minutes.

5. Get help pulling the dish out of the oven, but keep the oven on. Sprinkle the shredded coconut on the chicken. Do not stir or turn the chicken after the coconut is on it. Bake a final 10 minutes, or until the coconut is lightly browned.

Makes 8 to 10 Coconut-Curry Kookoo Chicken drumsticks.

COCONUT-CURRY KOOKOO CHICKEN WITH
SIMPLE RICE AND PEAS (PAGE 32)

LASAGNE JUMBLE

Lasagne Jumble

[*main*]

SUPPLIES

bowl, measuring spoons, measuring cups, whisk, baking spatula, 2.5- to 3.5-litre baking dish, can opener, foil (or lid of baking dish), oven mitts

INGREDIENTS

2 tbsp butter

2 tbsp plain flour

125 ml water

1 can (800 g) diced or crushed tomatoes

1 tsp white sugar

½ tsp dried oregano

½ tsp finely chopped garlic (from jar)

½ tsp salt

pinch of pepper

6 or 7 oven-ready lasagne noodles (six 25 cm long noodles or seven 18 cm long noodles)

250 ml cottage cheese

12 to 16 frozen meatballs (2.5 cm each)

8 tbsp pre-grated mozzarella or white cheddar cheese

This recipe uses pre-made meatballs, but you do the rest to make a cheese-topped pasta for supper.

1. Preheat the oven to 190°C/170°C fan/gas 5.

2. Place the butter in a microwave-safe bowl, then heat in the microwave at 50% power until melted (about 30 seconds). Remove the butter from the microwave and whisk in the flour until smooth. Use a baking spatula to scrape the mixture into the baking dish.

3. Use a whisk to gradually mix the water into the butter and flour mixture until smooth.

4. Switching back to the baking spatula, stir in the canned tomatoes, sugar, oregano, garlic, salt, and pepper.

5. Break the lasagne noodles into roughly 5 cm sections (it's okay if they are jagged and uneven) and add them to the baking dish. Stir well to moisten the noodles. Add the cottage cheese in dollops overtop. Stir until about half the cottage cheese is mixed into the tomato sauce mixture and half the cheese stays in white streaks. Push down any large noodles that poke out of the liquid, but don't worry if some stick up.

6. Use your fingers to press the meatballs into the noodle mixture, spacing them as evenly as possible; they do not need to be covered by the sauce and noodles. Wash your hands.

7. Cover the baking dish with a lid or foil. Get help putting it in the oven. Bake for 30 minutes.

8. Get help removing the dish from the oven and uncovering it. Put on oven mitts, or get help, to stir the Lasagna Jumble just to coat everything with sauce. Spread the mixture evenly in the dish. Sprinkle the top with the pre-grated cheese. Put back in the oven, uncovered, and bake for another 15 minutes until the cheese is melted.

Makes 4 servings.

Mozzarella Chicken

[main] [GF]

SUPPLIES

rimmed baking sheet, parchment paper, measuring spoons, measuring cups, 3 bowls, fork, ordinary teaspoon

INGREDIENTS

1 tbsp olive oil

5 tbsp plain flour (regular or gluten-free) (spoon in, level; see page 19)

½ tsp garlic salt

2 eggs

2 tbsp water

250 ml (1 cup) dry breadcrumbs (regular or gluten-free)

8 to 10 skinless, boneless chicken thighs

185 ml tomato sauce

12 tbsp pre-grated mozzarella cheese

The whole family will enjoy this breaded chicken. If you add salad and rolls on the side, it's a perfect supper for four.

1. Preheat the oven to 180°C/160°C fan/gas 4.

2. Line a rimmed baking sheet with parchment paper. Drizzle it with olive oil. Set aside.

3. Now you'll make an assembly line for breading the chicken. In one bowl, mix the flour and garlic salt. Next to this, in a second bowl, use a fork to beat the eggs and water. Finally, put the breadcrumbs in a third bowl. Now you're ready to coat the chicken.

4. If the chicken thighs are rolled up in the store package, unroll them. Coat two or three pieces at a time. First, roll the chicken in the flour mixture to coat all sides. Shake off the extra flour, then roll in the egg mixture to moisten all sides. Lift the pieces to let the extra egg drip off, then roll the chicken in the breadcrumbs to coat all sides. Throw out the stuff in the bowls.

5. Lay the pieces of chicken flat on the oiled parchment paper. Wash your hands.

6. Bake for 25 minutes.

7. Get help removing the baking sheet from the oven (but keep the oven on). Cool for about 5 minutes so you can work near the baking sheet without burning yourself.

8. Use an ordinary teaspoon to spread the tomato sauce on the chicken. Sprinkle the mozzarella cheese overtop.

9. Put the chicken back into the oven and bake for another 13 to 15 minutes until the cheese is melted.

Makes 8 to 10 pieces of Mozzarella Chicken.

MOZZARELLA CHICKEN

SEVEN SEAS SALMON WITH PARMESAN RISOTTO (PAGE 41)

Seven Seas Salmon

[main] [GF]

SUPPLIES

rimmed baking sheet, parchment paper, measuring spoons, bowl, ordinary teaspoon, kitchen scissors

INGREDIENTS

750 g salmon fillet (in 4 pieces or 1 large piece)

1 tsp olive oil

1 tsp packed brown sugar

1 tsp chilli powder

½ tsp lemon pepper

¼ tsp ground cumin

⅛ tsp salt

6 stalks chives, if you like

Salmon is delicious sprinkled with this "secret" blend of spices from all over the world.

1. Preheat the oven to 180°C/160°C fan/gas 4.

2. If the salmon is in one piece, get help cutting it into four pieces.

3. Line a rimmed baking sheet with parchment paper. Pour the olive oil into the middle of the parchment. Use your hands to roll the pieces of salmon in the olive oil, rubbing it onto all sides of the fish.

4. Place the salmon pieces—skin on the bottom, if there is skin—about 5 cm apart in the middle of the parchment. Wash your hands.

5. In a small bowl, mix the brown sugar, chilli powder, lemon pepper, cumin, and salt. Fill an ordinary teaspoon with the spice mixture; hold it over the salmon and gently tap the handle to let the spices fall evenly onto the fish. Use up all the spice mixture.

6. Bake on the middle rack of the oven. If the salmon is 2.5 cm thick (or more) at its thickest part, bake for 10 minutes, then get help to check if it is cooked through. Salmon is cooked when it turns a light creamy pink-orange colour. If the salmon is still too raw, put it back into the oven for another 2 minutes. If the salmon is less than 2.5 cm thick, check it at 8 minutes. Be careful not to overcook the fish.

7. While the salmon is cooking, use kitchen scissors to cut the chives into little pieces, if using. To make this go faster, hold the chives together in a bunch and cut through all of them at once.

8. After the salmon is cooked, get help putting it on dinner plates. Sprinkle the fish with the snipped chives and serve right away.

Makes 4 servings.

Every-Flavour Pork Chops

[*main*] [GF]

SUPPLIES

glass or ceramic baking dish just large enough to hold the pork in a single layer, baking spatula or spoon, measuring spoons, kitchen scissors

INGREDIENTS

1 tbsp firmly packed brown sugar

3 tbsp soy sauce

2 tbsp red wine vinegar

1 tbsp vegetable oil

2 tbsp runny honey

1 tsp finely chopped garlic (from jar)

½ tsp dried thyme

1 spring onion

6 to 8 boneless pork loins or bone-in pork chops (about 1 cm thick, up to 1 kg)

A little salty, a bit sweet, a touch of tanginess, and a hint of herbs. These saucy pork chops will perk up your taste buds!

1. Preheat the oven to 180°C/160°C fan/gas 4.

2. In the baking dish and using a baking spatula or spoon, mix the brown sugar, soy sauce, vinegar, oil, honey, garlic, and thyme. This is the marinade.

3. Use kitchen scissors to snip the green onion into little pieces, about the size of your fingernail, right into the marinade (throw away or compost the root).

4. Use your hands to put the pieces of pork in the marinade and turn to coat all sides. Wash your hands.

5. Bake, uncovered, on the middle rack of the oven for 15 to 20 minutes, or until the meat is cooked through. Get help checking that the meat is done. Serve with some juices from the baking dish spooned overtop.

Makes 4 servings.

EVERY-FLAVOUR PORK CHOPS WITH
CASHEW COUSCOUS (BLESS YOU!) (PAGE 27)

YOUR OWN BBQ-SAUCED CHICKEN

WITH BUTTERED GREEN BEANS (PAGE 40)

Your Own BBQ-Sauced Chicken

[main] [GF]

SUPPLIES

rimmed baking sheet, parchment paper, ordinary teaspoon, measuring spoons, pastry brush or cling film, measuring cups, bowl

INGREDIENTS

1 tsp vegetable oil

4 skinless, boneless chicken breasts

BBQ SAUCE

125 ml tomato sauce

1 tbsp runny honey

1 tsp white vinegar

½ tsp chilli powder

½ tsp brown sugar

¼ tsp ground cumin

¼ tsp Worcestershire sauce

The fun in this recipe is making your own BBQ sauce. From now on, when you see bottles of it in the store, you'll know the ingredients!

1. Preheat the oven to 190°C/170°C fan/gas 5.

2. Line a baking sheet with parchment paper. Use a pastry brush or a scrunched-up piece of cling film to rub the oil over the parchment. Place the chicken breasts on the oiled parchment, making sure the pieces don't touch.

3. To make your own BBQ sauce, use an ordinary teaspoon to mix the tomato sauce, honey, vinegar, chilli powder, brown sugar, cumin, and Worcestershire sauce in a bowl. Use the spoon to spread about half of the BBQ sauce on top of the chicken.

4. Bake for 20 minutes.

5. Get help removing the baking sheet from the oven and turning the chicken breasts over. Spoon the remaining BBQ sauce onto the second side of the chicken. Be careful not to touch the hot baking sheet. Bake for another 5 to 10 minutes. Get help removing the chicken and checking that it is cooked through.

Makes 4 servings.

your kitchen specials

Make your favourite meals and
snacks just the way you like them!

COCOA-KISSED BANANA OATMEAL

Cocoa-Kissed Banana Oatmeal

[*breakfast*]

SUPPLIES

1.5 litre glass or ceramic baking dish,
baking spatula or wooden spoon,
measuring cups, measuring spoons,
dinner knife, oven mitts

INGREDIENTS

250 ml (1 cup) rolled oats, traditional or
   quick-cooking (but not instant)
1 tbsp unsweetened cocoa powder
pinch of salt
375 ml warm tap water
⅛ tsp vanilla
1 banana
brown sugar or maple syrup and milk
   to serve

Bananas and cocoa are a perfect taste pairing.
The banana slices melt into the oatmeal as they
soften and sweeten in the oven.

1. Preheat the oven to 200°C/180°C fan/gas 6.

2. In a baking dish and using a baking spatula or wooden spoon, stir together the rolled oats, cocoa powder, and salt. Mix in the water and vanilla. Don't worry if the cocoa powder doesn't mix in completely at this point.

3. Peel the banana. Use a dinner knife to cut half of the banana into slices. Stir the slices into the oatmeal mixture. Save the other half of the banana for topping the oatmeal later.

4. Bake on the middle rack of the oven, uncovered, for 15 minutes, just until the water is absorbed into the oats.

5. Get help taking the dish out of the oven. Cool a few minutes until just warm, then get help or wear oven mitts to spoon the oatmeal into serving bowls and serve sprinkled with brown sugar or drizzled with maple syrup, a splash of milk and slices from the remaining half banana.

Makes 500 ml.

Piggies in Blankets

[lunch]

SUPPLIES

measuring spoons, drinking cup, measuring cups, cling film, bowl, whisk or fork, baking spatula, dinner knife, parchment paper, baking sheet, rolling pin, pizza wheel

INGREDIENTS

1½ tsp white sugar

½ tsp quick-rise yeast

125 ml very warm (but not hot) water (see "Yeast," page 19)

250 ml (1 cup) plain flour (spoon in, level; see page 19)

½ tsp baking powder

¼ tsp salt

1 egg white (see "Eggs," page 16)

2 tbsp vegetable oil

125 ml (½ cup) plain flour (spoon in, level)

1 tbsp plain flour

6 hot dog sausages

You might have baked these before from store-bought dough, but here's your chance to learn how to make piggies from scratch.

1. Put the sugar and yeast into a drinking cup. Add the warm water. Do not stir. Cover with cling film and let stand 10 minutes for the yeast to turn foamy.

2. Meanwhile, in a bowl, mix the flour, baking powder, and salt. Set aside.

3. Go back to the cup of foamy yeast after the yeast has risen for 10 minutes. Use a whisk or fork to beat the egg white and vegetable oil into the yeast. Use a baking spatula to scrape this wet mixture into the flour mixture. Stir into a loose dough until there is no dry flour left. Use a dinner knife to scrape sticky ingredients off the spatula. Cover the bowl with cling film and let the dough rise for 30 minutes in a warm spot.

4. Take this waiting time to cut two pieces of parchment paper the size of your baking sheet. Set aside.

5. After the dough has risen, sprinkle the remaining flour on it and stir until all the dry flour disappears. Cover the bowl again and let the dough rise for another 10 minutes in a warm spot.

6. Preheat the oven to 190°C/170°C fan/gas 5.

7. After the dough finishes the second rising, sprinkle 1 tbsp flour onto it (keep the dough in the bowl). Use your hands to squeeze the flour into the dough. The dough should be very stretchy but not stick to your hands. If it is too sticky, squeeze in another tablespoon of flour.

8. Roll the dough out of the bowl onto the middle of a piece of parchment paper. Cover the dough with the other piece of parchment. Use your rolling pin to roll the dough (keeping it between the paper) into a circle roughly 5 mm thick (see "Two-Stacked-Pound-Coins Rule," page 19).

CONTINUED ON NEXT PAGE

9. Remove the top piece of parchment paper. Use a pizza wheel to cut across the dough three times to make six triangular wedges.

10. Now you can wrap the sausages. Place each sausage on the wide end of a triangle of dough. Roll the dough around the sausage until you wrap up the pointy end. Wrap all six sausages. The ends of the sausages will stick out the ends of the rolled dough.

11. Line the baking sheet with the piece of parchment that is least crumpled. Place the piggies on it with the pointy end of the dough on the bottom so it won't unravel.

12. Bake on the middle rack of the oven for 18 to 20 minutes until golden. Cool until the piggies are just warm to the touch before eating.

Makes 6 Piggies in Blankets.

PIGGIES IN BLANKETS

Real Mac 'n' Cheddar Cheese

[lunch or supper]

SUPPLIES

2.5 litre glass or ceramic baking dish, baking spatula, measuring cups, measuring spoons, foil (or lid of baking dish), bowls, whisk, wooden spoon

INGREDIENTS

MACARONI

375 ml (1½ cups) uncooked elbow
  macaroni
1 tsp vegetable oil
580 ml warm tap water

CHEESE SAUCE

4 tbsp unsalted butter
3 tbsp plain flour
½ tsp dry mustard
½ tsp salt
½ tsp white sugar
¼ tsp onion powder
⅛ tsp chilli powder
250 ml milk
375 ml (1½ cups) pre-grated cheddar
  cheese

BREADCRUMB TOPPING

1 tbsp unsalted butter
8 tbsp dry breadcrumbs
pinch of salt

You can make real macaroni and cheese that does not come from a box!

1. Preheat the oven to 190°C/170°C fan/gas 5.

2. In the baking dish and using a baking spatula, mix the macaroni with the vegetable oil until the macaroni is well coated.

3. Pour the warm water onto the macaroni. Cover tightly with a lid or foil. Bake for 30 minutes. Get help taking it out of the oven. Keep covered for at least another 15 minutes. The macaroni softens some more and the baking dish cools off a bit.

4. Meanwhile, make the sauce. In a large microwave-safe bowl, melt the butter in the microwave at 50% power (about 1 minute). Use a whisk to mix in the flour until smooth. Then mix in the dry mustard, salt, sugar, onion powder, and chilli powder. Gradually whisk in the milk until smooth.

5. Heat the sauce in the microwave on high for 1 minute (or longer, but only 1 minute at a time so it doesn't foam over), until the sauce is bubbly and thickened. Get help removing the bowl from the microwave. Cool slightly so the bowl isn't too hot to touch.

6. Stir the cheddar into the sauce. The cheese does not need to be fully melted in right now. Set aside.

7. Next make the breadcrumb topping. In a large microwave-safe bowl, heat 1 tbsp unsalted butter in the microwave at 50% power until melted (about 30 seconds). Mix in the breadcrumbs and salt. Use the back of a wooden spoon to mash the breadcrumbs into the butter to break up lumps.

8. Get help uncovering the dish of macaroni (there should be some water left in the bottom of the dish). Using a baking spatula, scrape the cheese sauce onto the macaroni. Stir well. Spread the macaroni evenly in the dish. Sprinkle the breadcrumbs on top. Bake, uncovered, for about 20 minutes, or until the breadcrumbs are lightly golden.

Makes 750 ml.

REAL MAC 'N' CHEDDAR CHEESE

SPINACH AND MUSHROOM FRITTATA

Spinach and Mushroom Frittata

[lunch or supper] [GF]

SUPPLIES

rimmed baking sheet, parchment paper, pastry brush or cling film, measuring spoons, 23 cm glass, ceramic, or non-stick metal pie tin, measuring cups, bowl, whisk, ordinary teaspoon

INGREDIENTS

2 tsp olive oil for pie tin

250 ml (1 cup) loosely packed baby spinach leaves

125 ml (½ cup) pre-sliced button mushrooms

1 tbsp olive oil

4 tbsp milk

2 tbsp plain flour (regular or gluten-free)

5 eggs

1 tbsp dried onion flakes

½ tsp finely chopped garlic (from jar)

¼ tsp salt

pinch of pepper

4 tbsp pre-grated cheddar cheese

A frittata is a kind of omelette baked in a pan. Baking the spinach first shrinks it down to fit into the pie tin. A great recipe to make as a special brunch for a family member's birthday.

1. Preheat the oven to 190°C/170°C fan/gas 5.

2. Line a baking sheet with parchment paper.

3. Use a pastry brush or a scrunched-up piece of cling film to rub 2 tsp olive oil onto the bottom and sides of the pie tin. Set aside.

4. Put the spinach, mushrooms, and 1 tbsp olive oil in a large bowl and mix with your hands until well coated. Spread the mixture out on the parchment-lined baking sheet, then wash and dry your hands. Put the baking sheet into the oven and bake for 10 minutes, or until the mushrooms are shrunken in size and the spinach is wilted (don't worry if some leaves turn crispy; they're delicious mixed into the frittata). Remove from the oven and cool (keep the oven on).

5. In the bowl you used for the spinach and mushrooms, whisk the milk and flour until smooth. Then whisk in the eggs, onion flakes, garlic, salt, and pepper. Stir in the cheddar cheese and cooled spinach and mushrooms. Pour the mixture into the pie tin. Use an ordinary teaspoon to gently spread out the cheese, spinach, and mushrooms.

6. Get help putting the pie tin onto the middle rack of the oven. Bake for 25 minutes, or until the frittata puffs up (it will flatten after it comes out of the oven). Cool for a few minutes before slicing into wedges to serve.

Makes 4 kid-sized or 2 adult-sized servings.

Hula Hawaiian Pizza

[lunch or supper]

SUPPLIES

measuring spoons, drinking cup, measuring cups, cling film, bowl, baking spatula, dinner knife, baking sheet, parchment paper, wooden spoon, ordinary teaspoon, kitchen scissors

INGREDIENTS

CRUST

1 tsp quick-rise yeast

½ tsp white sugar

185 ml very warm (but not hot) water (see "Yeast," page 19)

375 ml (1½ cups) plain flour (spoon in, level; see page 19)

½ tsp salt

olive or vegetable oil for your hands

TOPPINGS

160 ml tomato sauce

1 or 2 slices ham

10 tbsp pre-grated mozzarella cheese

handful fresh or canned pineapple chunks

Make your own pizza parlor crust, then top it with ham and juicy pineapple.

1. To make the crust, put the yeast and sugar in a drinking cup. Measure out the warm water and add it to the yeast and sugar. Do not stir. Cover with cling film and let stand 10 minutes for the yeast to turn foamy.

2. Meanwhile, in a large bowl and using a baking spatula, mix the flour and salt. Use the baking spatula to scrape the foamy yeast into the flour mixture. Stir into a smooth, sticky dough that has no dry flour left in it. Scrape sticky ingredients off the spatula with a dinner knife. Cover the bowl with cling film and set in a warm place to rise for 30 minutes.

3. Preheat the oven to 200°C/180°C fan/gas 6.

4. Line a baking sheet with parchment paper.

5. You can make two small pizzas or one bigger one on the baking sheet. If you make two smaller ones, the crusts will be crispier.

6. Use a wooden spoon to scoop out either two equal-sized blobs of dough or one big blob onto the baking sheet. Let the dough rest for 10 minutes. Believe it or not, letting the dough sit untouched for a while makes it easier to press out later.

7. Rub some oil onto your hands. Here's where the hard work begins. Press the dough with your fingers into one or two roughly round shapes about 6 mm thick (see "Two-Stacked-Pound-Coins Rule," page 19). It is stretchy dough and might spring back as you flatten it, but keep working and the dough will spread out. Don't worry if you end up with an odd shape.

8. Bake the dough for 15 minutes, or until it begins to turn golden. Get help taking the sheet out of the oven (keep the oven on). Cool the baking sheet until just warm so you don't burn yourself adding toppings.

CONTINUED ON NEXT PAGE

9 If you are making two pizzas, pour half of the tomato sauce onto one crust and half onto the other, or pour all the tomato sauce onto the one big crust. Use the back of an ordinary teaspoon to spread the sauce on the crust, leaving about 1 cm at the edges.

10 Use kitchen scissors to cut the ham into bite-sized pieces. Sprinkle the ham, cheese, and pineapple pieces on top of the pizza(s).

11 Put the baking sheet back in the oven for another 10 minutes, or until the cheese is melted and the edges of the crusts are golden. Eat while warm.

Makes 2 smaller or 1 larger Hula Hawaiian Pizza.

HULA HAWAIIAN PIZZA

Hocus Pocus Pizza

[lunch or supper] [GF]

SUPPLIES

rimmed baking sheet, parchment paper, measuring spoons, drinking cup, measuring cups, cling film, sieve, bowl, baking spatula, dinner knife, ordinary teaspoon, pastry brush

INGREDIENTS

CRUST

1 tsp white sugar

1 tsp quick-rise yeast

250 ml very warm (but not hot) water (see "Yeast," page 19)

250 ml (1 cup) white rice flour (regular, not glutinous) (spoon in, level; see page 19)

125 ml (½ cup) potato starch (spoon in, level)

5 tbsp cornflour (spoon in, level)

1 tsp baking powder

½ tsp salt

¼ tsp unflavoured gelatin powder

1 tbsp vegetable oil

TOPPINGS

1 tsp vegetable oil

185 ml tomato sauce

handful pepperoni slices or other favourite toppings

8 tbsp pre-grated white cheddar cheese

8 tbsp pre-grated mozzarella cheese

This is a fantastic gluten-free pizza for kids who don't eat wheat flour. Unlike other crusts, this one is made by an unusual method of pouring a batter, not pressing dough. The batter bakes into a crispy-edged but tender crust. Magic!

1. Preheat the oven to 230°C/210°C fan/gas 8

2. Line a baking sheet with parchment paper.

3. Put the sugar and yeast into a drinking cup. Add the warm water. Do not stir. Cover with cling film and let stand 10 minutes for the yeast to turn foamy.

4. Sift the rice flour, potato starch, cornflour, baking powder, and salt into a large bowl. Add the gelatin powder. Mix well with a baking spatula.

5. Go back to your foamy yeast. Using the baking spatula, scrape it into the flour mixture. Add the 1 tbsp vegetable oil. Mix into a thick batter, scraping sticky ingredients off the spatula with a dinner knife. It is not a dough. It should look like very thick pancake batter. If it is too runny, mix in another tablespoon or two of rice flour.

6. Scrape the batter onto the parchment-lined baking sheet and let it spread out on its own. It will stiffen and stop spreading after a few seconds. Use your baking spatula to gently spread the batter to 6 mm thickness.

7. Bake on the middle rack of the oven for 25 minutes (the crust does not turn golden). Get help taking the crust out of the oven (but keep the oven on). Let the crust and baking sheet cool slightly so you don't burn yourself working with the crust.

8. Use a pastry brush to brush 1 tsp vegetable oil around the outside 2.5 cm of the crust. This helps it turn golden at the edges.

CONTINUED ON NEXT PAGE

9 Using an ordinary teaspoon, scoop the tomato sauce onto the crust and spread it with the back of the spoon almost to the edges. Sprinkle on your toppings and cheeses.

10 Bake on the middle rack of the oven for 5 to 6 minutes, or until the cheese melts.

Serves 4 kids as a snack or light lunch.

HOCUS POCUS PIZZA

Gobble-Up Turkey Burgers

[lunch or supper] [GF]

SUPPLIES

rimmed baking sheet, parchment paper, measuring spoons, kitchen scissors, bowl, measuring cups

INGREDIENTS

2 tbsp dried cranberries

500 g minced turkey (or chicken)

1 egg

4 tbsp dry breadcrumbs (regular or gluten-free)

1 tsp dried parsley

1 tsp onion powder

½ tsp chilli powder

¼ tsp salt

pinch of nutmeg

pinch of pepper

5 burger buns (regular or gluten-free)

your choice of toppings such as lettuce, tomato, cheese

If you like holiday turkey, you'll love these burgers any time of year. If you have lots of time you can also make the buns (see page 78), but it's totally fine to buy them.

1. Preheat the oven to 190°C/170°C fan/gas 5.

2. Line a rimmed baking sheet with parchment paper.

3. Use kitchen scissors to cut the cranberries into small pieces (each berry into three or four pieces). Put the pieces in a large bowl.

4. Into the same bowl, add the minced turkey, egg, breadcrumbs, parsley, onion powder, chilli powder, salt, nutmeg, and pepper.

5. Use your hands to mix everything well. Yes, it will feel squishy, but you need to mix until the spices are spread out evenly. Divide the mixture into five equal-sized blobs. Pat each one into a ball, then gently flatten into 2 cm thick patties. Place on the parchment-lined sheet. Wash your hands.

6. Bake on the middle rack of the oven for 10 minutes. Get help turning the patties over, then bake for another 10 minutes. Place each patty into a hamburger bun and add toppings.

Makes 5 Gobble-Up Turkey Burgers.

GOBBLE-UP TURKEY BURGERS AND
BURGER BUNS (PAGE 78)

Lovin' Oven Hamburgers

[lunch or supper] [GF]

SUPPLIES

rimmed baking sheet, parchment paper, measuring cups, measuring spoons, bowl

INGREDIENTS

500 g minced beef

1 egg

4 tbsp dry breadcrumbs (regular or gluten-free)

2 tsp dried onion flakes

2 tsp ketchup

¼ tsp garlic salt

pinch of pepper

4 or 5 burger buns (regular or gluten-free)

your choice of toppings such as lettuce, tomato, cheese

Making burgers in the oven lets you get a bunch of patties ready at once! If you have lots of time you can also make the buns (see page 78), but it's totally fine to buy them.

1. Preheat the oven to 190°C/170°C fan/gas 5.

2. Line a rimmed baking sheet with parchment paper. Set aside.

3. Place the minced beef, egg, breadcrumbs, onion flakes, ketchup, garlic salt, and pepper in a large bowl. Use your hands to mix everything well.

4. Divide the mixture into four or five equal-sized blobs. Pat each one into a ball, then flatten into 2 cm thick patties. Place on the lined baking sheet.

5. Bake on the middle rack of the oven for 15 minutes. Get help turning the patties over, then bake for another 10 minutes. Tuck into hamburger buns and add toppings.

Makes 4 or 5 Lovin' Oven Hamburgers.

LOVIN' OVEN HAMBURGERS AND
BURGER BUNS (PAGE 78)

Burger Buns

[lunch or supper]

SUPPLIES

measuring spoons, drinking cups, measuring cups, cling film, bowl, baking spatula, fork, dinner knife, baking sheet, parchment paper, pizza wheel, pastry brush, knife (for helper)

INGREDIENTS

1½ tsp white sugar

½ tsp quick-rise yeast

125 ml very warm (but not hot) water (see "Yeast," page 19)

375 ml (1½ cups) plain flour (spoon in, level; see page 19)

¾ tsp baking powder

¼ tsp salt

1 egg white (see "Eggs," page 16)

2 tbsp vegetable oil

4 tbsp plain flour (spoon in, level)

flour for your fingers

1 tsp milk

½ tsp sesame seeds, if you like

PICTURED ON PAGES 75 AND 77

You can make your own burger buns! But make these on a day when you have extra time because they need almost an hour to rise. Eat them while they're fresh because they won't keep overnight. The Gobble-Up Turkey Burgers (page 74) or the Lovin' Oven Hamburgers (page 76) are great with these buns. Or use them to make sandwiches!

1. Measure out the sugar and yeast into a drinking cup. Add the warm water. Do not stir. Cover with cling film and set aside for 10 minutes to let the yeast turn foamy.

2. In a large bowl and using a baking spatula, mix the flour, baking powder (measure out ½ tsp and ¼ tsp to make ¾ tsp), and salt. Set aside.

3. In another drinking cup, use a fork to beat the egg white and vegetable oil until frothy. Use a baking spatula to scrape this into the flour mixture. Scrape the foamy yeast into the bowl, too. Stir into a loose dough, scraping the sticky ingredients off the spatula with a dinner knife. Cover the bowl with cling film and let rise for 30 minutes in a warm spot.

4. After the dough has risen, sprinkle the 4 tbsp flour on the dough and use your hands to squeeze it into the dough until all the dry flour disappears.

5. Cover the bowl again and let rise for another 20 minutes.

6. Line a baking sheet with parchment paper.

7. After the dough has risen again, tip the bowl on its side on the parchment, flour your fingertips, and lightly roll the dough out of the bowl onto the parchment. You want to keep as much air in the dough as possible, so please don't squish it. Pretend you're handling a delicate egg!

CONTINUED ON NEXT PAGE

(8) Use a pizza wheel or dinner knife to slice the dough into four equal pieces. Using your hands, gently pat each piece into a ball—or roughly a ball—and set it back on the parchment. Remember, don't squish out the air, and try to keep the balls puffy and rounded on top if you can. Place the four pieces of dough about 3 inches (8 cm) apart on the parchment.

(9) Use a pastry brush to lightly brush the dough with milk. Sprinkle with sesame seeds, if you like. Set aside to rise just a little more while your oven heats up.

(10) Preheat the oven to 190°C/170°C fan/gas 5.

(11) Bake on the middle rack of the oven for 27 to 28 minutes, or until golden. Wow! You just made your own hamburger buns! Get help slicing each bun in half crosswise so they can hold patties or sandwich fillings.

Makes 4 Burger Buns.

Fin-Tastic Fish Fillets

[supper] [GF]

SUPPLIES

rimmed baking sheet, parchment paper, measuring spoons, bowls, fork or small whisk, measuring cups, plate, knife (for helper)

INGREDIENTS

1 tbsp vegetable oil

1 egg white (see "Eggs," page 16)

5 tbsp plain yogurt

1 tsp vegetable oil

125 ml (½ cup) dry breadcrumbs (regular or gluten-free)

3 tbsp pre-grated Parmesan cheese

1 tsp lemon pepper

¼ tsp salt

5 tbsp plain flour (regular or gluten-free) (spoon in, level; see page 19)

375 g firm white fish fillets such as tilapia, haddock, or catfish

Fresh fish is delicious. Here's how to make a lightly breaded crust for it.

1. Preheat the oven to 190°C/170°C fan/gas 5.

2. Line a rimmed baking sheet with parchment paper. Drizzle with 1 tbsp vegetable oil. Set aside.

3. Now you need to make an assembly line for breading the fish. First, in a big bowl, use a fork or small whisk to beat the egg white, yogurt, and 1 tsp oil until smooth. In another big bowl, mix the breadcrumbs, Parmesan cheese, lemon pepper, and salt. Finally, spread out the flour on a plate.

4. Get help cutting each fish fillet into three or four large pieces.

5. Begin by rolling the pieces of fish in the flour. Make sure you cover all sides of the fish. Next, roll the floured fish in the yogurt mixture. Finally, roll the fish in the breadcrumb mixture. Lay the fish on the parchment paper, making sure you lay the pieces on some of the drizzled oil. Wash your hands. Throw away the stuff in the bowls and plate.

6. Bake for 8 minutes. Get help turning the fish over, then bake for another 5 minutes, or until golden.

Makes 2 to 3 kid-sized servings.

FIN-TASTIC FISH FILLETS

REALLY BIG CHICKEN MEATBALLS

Really Big Chicken Meatballs

[*supper*] [GF]

SUPPLIES

measuring spoons, large glass
or ceramic baking dish, measuring
cups, bowls, fork, wooden spoon,
pastry brush

INGREDIENTS

2 tsp vegetable oil

1 egg

2 tbsp milk

1 slice sandwich bread (brown or
white) (regular or gluten-free)

2 tbsp pre-grated Parmesan cheese

1 tbsp dried onion flakes

1 tbsp ketchup

1 tsp dried oregano

1 tsp dried parsley

¼ tsp salt

generous pinch of pepper

500 g minced chicken

2 tbsp BBQ sauce (use bottled kind or
see page 59 if you want to make your
own and use some for this recipe)

These large meatballs are big on flavour, too.
They're great to eat with pasta or bread.

1. Preheat the oven to 200°C/180°C fan/gas 6.

2. Drizzle the oil into the bottom of the baking dish. Set aside.

3. Have ready a big bowl of cold water for dipping your hands. Set aside.

4. In another large bowl, beat the egg and milk with a fork. Add the bread, turning it over to soak both sides. Let the bread turn mushy, then use a wooden spoon or your hands to break up the bread into a lumpy paste. (Wash your hands if necessary.)

5. Stir the Parmesan cheese, onion flakes, ketchup, oregano, parsley, salt, and pepper into the mushy bread mixture. Add the minced chicken to the bowl, then use your hands to mix everything up. Don't be timid. You have to squish it to mix everything!

6. Measure out 5 tbsp of the chicken mixture for each meatball. Pat it into a ball, and set it in the baking dish. The mixture is soft and sticky, so dip your hands into the bowl of cold water as you form the meatballs so the mixture doesn't stick to your hands. Make 7 meatballs, then wash your hands.

7. Bake on the middle rack of the oven for 30 minutes. Get help removing the baking dish from the oven, then brush the BBQ sauce onto the meatballs. Bake for another 5 minutes.

Makes 7 Really Big Chicken Meatballs.

LETTUCE WRAPS WITH CRUMBLED ASIAN PORK

Lettuce Wraps with Crumbled Asian Pork [*supper*] [GF]

SUPPLIES

rimmed baking sheet, parchment paper, bowls, measuring spoons, kitchen scissors, oven mitts, wooden spoon, colander, paper towel

INGREDIENTS

375 g minced pork

1 egg white (see "Eggs," page 16)

2 tbsp oyster sauce

1 tsp finely chopped garlic (from jar)

1 tsp soy sauce

1 tsp vegetable oil

pinch of pepper

2 spring onions

6 Butterhead lettuce leaves

TOPPINGS

diced peppers (get help cutting)

handful fresh bean sprouts

handful matchstick carrots

2 tbsp pre-chopped roasted peanuts
  or 1 tbsp sesame seeds

These are like tacos, except the wrapper is a lettuce leaf!

1. Preheat the oven to 190°C/170°C fan/gas 5.

2. Line a rimmed baking sheet with parchment paper.

3. In a large bowl, add the minced pork, egg white, oyster sauce, garlic, soy sauce, vegetable oil, and pepper. Use kitchen scissors to snip the green onion into little pieces into the bowl (throw away or compost the roots).

4. Use your hands to mush together everything in the bowl until it is well mixed. Don't be shy about getting your hands in there! Pinch off walnut-sized blobs of the pork mixture and drop them all over the parchment-lined sheet. Wash your hands.

5. Roast the pork on the middle rack of the oven for 10 minutes. Get help removing the baking sheet from the oven (keep the oven on). Cool for a few minutes until you can safely work with the sheet.

6. Put on an oven mitt to hold the baking sheet while you use a wooden spoon to break up the pork into smaller pieces, turning them over, too (you can also get help to do this). Put the baking sheet back into the oven to roast for another 10 minutes, or until the pork begins to brown.

7. Meanwhile, use a colander to wash the lettuce leaves, then pat them dry with a paper towel.

8. To serve, fill each leaf with spoonfuls of the warm crumbled pork. Add your choice of toppings. Roll up the lettuce around the filling to eat.

Makes 6 Lettuce Wraps with Crumbled Asian Pork.

Tangy Chicken Wings

[snack] [GF]

SUPPLIES

1 or 2 rimmed baking sheet(s), parchment paper, bowls, baking spatula, measuring spoons, measuring cups, heatproof tongs

INGREDIENTS

SINGLE BATCH

MARINADE

1 tbsp cider vinegar

2 tsp soy sauce

1 tsp vegetable oil

½ tsp chilli powder

½ tsp finely chopped garlic (from jar) or ¼ tsp garlic powder

500 g chicken wings (about 12 pieces)

GLAZE

2 tbsp ketchup

1 tbsp runny honey

1 tsp lemon juice or ½ tsp cider vinegar

⅛ tsp chilli powder

⅛ tsp Worcestershire sauce

These are tasty treats to have once in a while. If you want to have more to share with your family or friends, make the double batch (see facing page). Follow the same steps for either quantity of wings.

① Preheat the oven to 190°C/170°C fan/gas 5.

② Line a baking sheet with parchment paper (line 2 baking sheets if you're making the double batch).

③ In a large bowl and using a baking spatula, mix the marinade ingredients. Add the chicken wings and mix them around to coat them with the marinade. The easiest way to do this is to use your hands! Put the wings on the parchment-lined baking sheet(s). Throw away the leftover marinade so you don't get it mixed up with the glaze you'll make later. Wash your hands.

④ Roast the wings on the middle rack of the oven for 35 minutes for the single batch or 45 minutes for the double batch, or until they begin to brown. Get help removing the baking sheet(s) from the oven and checking if the wings are cooked through. If they are not done, return them to the oven for about 5 more minutes and check again.

⑤ While the wings are roasting, make the glaze. In a large, clean bowl, use a clean baking spatula to mix the glaze ingredients.

⑥ When the wings are finished roasting, use heatproof tongs to put the cooked wings into the bowl of glaze. Stir to coat the wings with glaze. Eat while warm.

Makes about 12 Tangy Chicken Wings (or about 24 in a double batch).

INGREDIENTS

DOUBLE BATCH

MARINADE

2 tbsp cider vinegar

1 tbsp soy sauce

2 tsp vegetable oil

1 tsp chilli powder

1 tsp finely chopped garlic (from jar) or
  ½ tsp garlic powder

1 kg chicken wings (about
  24 pieces)

GLAZE

4 tbsp ketchup

2 tbsp runny honey

1 tbsp lemon juice or 1 tsp
  cider vinegar

¼ tsp chilli powder

¼ tsp Worcestershire sauce

TANGY CHICKEN WINGS

Soft Twisted Pepperoni Breadsticks

[snack]

SUPPLIES

measuring spoons, drinking cup, measuring cups, cling film, bowl, sieve, kitchen scissors, pizza wheel, baking spatula, dinner knife, baking sheet, parchment paper, work board, pastry brush

INGREDIENTS

4 tsp white sugar

1 tsp quick-rise yeast

5 tbsp very warm (but not hot) water (see "Yeast," page 19)

2 tbsp soft unsalted butter (see "Butter," page 16)

375 ml (1½ cups) plain flour (spoon in, level; see page 19)

1 tsp chilli powder

1 tsp garlic salt

½ tsp dried oregano

½ tsp onion powder

20 pepperoni slices

1 egg

1 egg yolk (see "Eggs," page 16)

2 tbsp plain flour, plus more for dusting

5 tbsp tomato sauce

These are delicious warm from the oven as a snack, or served with a bowl of soup.

1. Put the sugar and yeast into a drinking cup. Add the warm water and lump of butter. Do not stir. Cover with cling film and set aside for 10 minutes to let the yeast turn foamy and the butter soften or melt.

2. In a large bowl, sift in the flour, chilli powder, garlic salt, oregano, and onion powder. Mix well.

3. Use kitchen scissors or a pizza wheel to cut the pepperoni slices into small pieces (about the size of your fingernail). Fill a 125 ml (½ cup) measuring cup with pepperoni pieces (you might not use up all of the pepperoni) and mix them into the flour mixture.

4. Using a baking spatula, scrape the yeast mixture into the flour mixture. Add the egg and egg yolk. Mix until no dry flour is left and the mixture turns into a soft dough. Use a dinner knife to scrape sticky ingredients off the spatula.

5. Cover the bowl with cling film and let the dough rise for 30 minutes in a warm spot.

6. Line a baking sheet with parchment paper. Preheat the oven to 180°C/160°C fan/gas 4.

7. Uncover the bowl of risen dough. Sprinkle on the 2 tbsp flour and stir or squeeze it into the dough until no dry flour is left. Dust your work board with flour. Tip the bowl of dough on its side and roll the dough out onto the floured board.

8. Flour your hands and pat the dough down into a 1 cm thick slab. It doesn't matter what the shape is, but aim for a rough rectangle about 15 × 23 cm.

9. Use a pizza wheel to cut the dough into strips roughly the size of hot dog sausages, about 15 cm long and 2 cm wide.

10. To give each strip of dough a swirly look, pick up each one and hold it at both ends.

CONTINUED ON NEXT PAGE

Twist one end around three or four times to make the strip look like twisty licorice. Place the strips on the parchment. The dough is very stretchy so don't worry if the sticks aren't perfect.

11 Use a pastry brush to brush the sticks with tomato sauce.

12 Bake on the middle rack of the oven for about 22 minutes, or until the breadsticks are puffy and the tomato sauce turns orange.

Makes 12 Soft Twisted Pepperoni Breadsticks.

Munchy Crunchy Crackers

[snack]

SUPPLIES

baking sheet, parchment paper, bowls, measuring cups, measuring spoons, baking spatula, dinner knife, rolling pin, fork, pizza wheel, cooling rack (the metal kind for cooling cakes)

INGREDIENTS

250 ml (1 cup) plain flour (spoon in, level; see page 19)

50 ml (¼ cup) whole wheat flour (spoon in, level)

½ tsp chilli powder

½ tsp dry mustard

½ tsp white sugar

5 tbsp milk

2 tbsp butter

It's amazing to make your own crackers! These taste so good on their own, but you can also eat them with cheese, if you like. You will need a helper with the baking step.

1. Preheat the oven to 180°C/160°C fan/gas 4.

2. Cut three sheets of parchment paper, each the size of your baking sheet. Set aside.

3. In a bowl, mix the two kinds of flour, chilli powder, dry mustard (be sure to use the back of a spoon to mash out any lumps), and sugar. Set aside.

4. In a microwave-safe bowl, heat the milk and butter in the microwave at 50% power until the butter is melted (about 1 minute).

5. Pour the milk mixture into the flour mixture. Use a baking spatula to scrape all the milk mixture into the flour bowl. Mix the ingredients into a dough, scraping sticky ingredients off the spatula with a dinner knife. When the dough gets too stiff to stir—keeping the dough in the bowl—use your hands to squeeze the dough against the crumbly bits and dry flour in the bottom of the bowl to work them into the dough.

6. Use a dinner knife to cut the dough into two equal-sized pieces. Put the first piece between two of the sheets of parchment paper you cut earlier. Put your rolling pin on the top sheet of parchment and roll out the dough to 2 mm (see "£2-Coin Rule," page 17). To make excellent crisp crackers, it is very important to roll the dough that thin. First roll across the whole piece of dough to flatten it, then make it even thinner by rolling from the middle of the dough out to the edges. Press down hard. And just when you think it's thin enough, roll it out again and check against the quarter coin. The dough puffs up a lot as it bakes.

CONTINUED ON PAGE 92

MUNCHY CRUNCHY CRACKERS

Munchy Crunchy Crackers (cont'd)

7. Peel off the top sheet of parchment. Prick the rolled dough every 2.5 cm with a fork. Use the pizza wheel to cut a checkerboard pattern into it. The squares should have about 4 cm sides. *Don't pull apart the squares of dough.* Leave them exactly where you cut them, touching in rows. Slide the parchment paper—with the dough on it—onto a baking sheet. Bake for 15 minutes.

8. While the first batch bakes, roll out the second piece of dough between two pieces of parchment, prick and cut it the same way as the first. Bake this batch the same way as the first batch (either use a second baking sheet or cool off the first one and use it again). Keep the oven on after baking the second batch. You will still need to bake all the crackers again to crisp them.

9. Remove the baked crackers and parchment from the baking sheet. Put a cooling rack on the baking sheet. Pull apart the crackers into squares and place them on the cooling rack.

10. Put the baking sheet—holding the cooling rack and crackers—in the oven. Bake another 10 minutes or until the crackers begin to brown. Ask a helper to remove the browned crackers and put crackers that aren't ready yet back in the oven for a few more minutes until they are also hard and crunchy.

Makes about 36 Munchy Crunchy Crackers.

Tortilla Corn Chips

[snack] [GF]

SUPPLIES

baking sheet, parchment paper, bowl, measuring cups, measuring spoons, cup or small bowl, baking spatula, dinner knife, rolling pin, kitchen scissors

INGREDIENTS

250 ml (1 cup) masa harina flour, also called "instant corn masa mix" (spoon in, level; see page 19)

1 tsp chilli powder

¼ tsp ground cumin

¼ tsp salt

pinch of black pepper

160 ml water

1 tbsp unsalted butter

tomato salsa or guacamole for dipping, if you like

You won't believe you made these at home! They look just like the ones you buy. Masa harina is a kind of flour made from corn. It's also called "instant corn masa mix" and is sold in many supermarkets and speciality food stores. Don't use any other flour for these super crunchy chips.

1. Preheat the oven to 180°C/160°C fan/gas 4.

2. Line a baking sheet with parchment paper. Also cut two 18 cm squares of parchment.

3. In a bowl, mix the masa harina flour, chilli powder, cumin, salt, and pepper. Set aside.

4. Place the water and butter in a microwave-safe cup or small bowl. Heat in the microwave on high until the butter is melted (about 30 seconds). Pour into the flour mixture. Stir with a baking spatula to make a dough. Use a dinner knife to scrape sticky ingredients off the spatula. When the dough is too stiff to stir, use your hands to squeeze the flour into the dough until no more dry flour can be seen.

5. Pinch off walnut-sized pieces of dough, roll into balls, and place each ball—one at a time—between the two squares of parchment paper you cut earlier. Roll each ball into roughly a 12.5 cm round shape 2 mm thick (see "£2-Coin Rule," page 17). Be sure to roll right over the edges of the dough to make it all the same thickness. Make sure the dough rounds are very thin— as thin as the tortilla chips you'd buy—or the chips won't be crunchy.

6. Remove the top square of parchment. Peel off the dough rounds from the remaining piece of parchment and place them on the parchment-lined baking sheet. Repeat rolling rounds of dough until you've filled up the baking sheet. Keep the rounds a little apart. They don't look like tortilla chips yet, but be patient.

CONTINUED ON PAGE 95

TORTILLA CORN CHIPS

Tortilla Corn Chips (cont'd)

7. Bake the dough rounds for 10 minutes. Remove from the oven (but keep the oven on) and let the dough cool off until you can handle it. Use kitchen scissors to cut across the rounds (they will be soft enough to cut easily) into four triangles each—or six triangles for slightly bigger rounds. Set these "chips" aside as you continue to roll and bake the rest of the dough by repeating steps 5, 6, and 7, until all the dough is baked in rounds and cut up into chips. You'll have a pile of corn chips on your work board now.

8. Reduce the oven temperature to 170°C/150°C fan/gas 3.

9. After the oven has reached the lower temperature, spread all the chips onto the parchment-lined baking sheet. Bake for 10 to 20 minutes, or until the chips are curled and crunchy. The time varies because of the size of your chips. Watch them closely through the oven window (or check often if you don't have a window) so you can see when they begin to brown. Cool. Eat with tomato salsa or guacamole, if you like.

Makes 3 big handfuls of Tortilla Corn Chips.

Parmesan Puffs

[snack] [GF]

SUPPLIES

pastry brush or cling film, mini-muffin tin (12 holes), bowls, measuring spoons, wooden spoon, measuring cups, baking spatula, ordinary teaspoon, dinner knife

INGREDIENTS

soft butter for muffin tin

3 tbsp plain flour (regular or gluten-free)

2 tbsp finely pre-grated Parmesan cheese

¾ tsp white sugar

¼ tsp garlic powder

¼ tsp dry mustard

big pinch of salt

tiny pinch of cayenne pepper, if you like

125 ml (½ cup) cream cheese

125 ml (½ cup) ricotta cheese

1 egg yolk (see "Eggs," page 16)

These taste like cheesy little soft, creamy quiches, but without crusts.

1. Preheat the oven to 180°C/160°C fan/gas 4.

2. Use a pastry brush or a scrunched-up piece of cling film to generously butter 12 mini-muffin cups. Set aside.

3. In a bowl, mix the flour, Parmesan cheese, sugar, garlic powder, dry mustard, salt, and, if you like, cayenne pepper (wash your fingers after touching the cayenne). Set aside.

4. In a microwave-safe bowl, heat the cream cheese at 50% power to soften it (about 1 minute). Use the back of a wooden spoon to cream together the cream cheese and ricotta, then mix in the egg yolk until smooth.

5. Use a baking spatula to gradually stir the flour mixture into the cheese mixture. Mix into a thick, smooth batter. Scrape the sticky ingredients off the spatula with a dinner knife to make sure everything is well blended.

6. Use an ordinary teaspoon to scoop the batter into the 12 mini-muffin cups. Fill each cup up to the rim. You might even get an extra one or two. Use your finger to push the batter off the spoon into the cups. It doesn't matter if the batter is bumpy and uneven on top.

7. Bake on the middle rack of the oven for 30 minutes, or until the puffs are golden and, well, puffed! Cool until slightly warm before lifting the puffs out of the cups using the tip of a dinner knife.

Makes about 12 Parmesan Puffs.

PARMESAN PUFFS

your own bakery

Be a pastry chef! Dazzle everyone
with amazing breads, cakes, and pies!

Fresh Lemon Cupcakes

SUPPLIES

paper cupcake liners (mini or regular size), cupcake tin(s) (20 mini or 8 regular holes), bowls, sieve, measuring cups, measuring spoons, wooden spoon, knife (for helper), reamer, baking spatula, dinner knife, ordinary teaspoon, cooling rack

INGREDIENTS

250 ml (1 cup) plain flour (spoon in, level; see page 19)

1 tsp baking powder

¼ tsp baking soda

pinch of salt

5 tbsp ricotta cheese

5 tbsp soft unsalted butter (see Butter, page 16)

185 ml (¾ cup) white sugar

1 egg

3 tbsp cream or milk

1 tsp vanilla extract

3 tbsp fresh lemon juice (from 1 lemon)

Fresh Lemon Double-Glaze (see page 102)

These yummy treats are lightly lemony and double-brushed with a tart sugar glaze. Make these as mini or regular-sized cupcakes.

1. Preheat the oven to 180°C/160°C fan/gas 4.

2. Place paper liners in either 20 mini or 8 regular cupcake cups. Set aside.

3. Sift the flour, baking powder, baking soda, and salt into a bowl. Mix well and set aside.

4. In a large bowl, use the back of a wooden spoon to cream together the ricotta and butter until blended, then cream in the sugar, egg, cream or milk, and vanilla. Set aside.

5. Get help cutting a lemon in half and juicing the fruit on a reamer. Use an ordinary teaspoon to scoop the seeds out of the juice. Measure out 3 tbsp lemon juice and stir it into the butter mixture.

6. Add the flour mixture to the butter mixture. Use a baking spatula to mix just until you don't see dry flour anymore. Scrape sticky ingredients off the spatula with a dinner knife.

7. Use an ordinary teaspoon to scoop up spoonfuls of batter. Use your finger to push the batter into the cupcake liners. Try not to spill batter outside the liners. You should be able to fill either 20 mini or 8 regular cupcake cups about three-quarters full.

8. Bake on the middle rack of the oven for about 18 minutes for mini cupcakes and 25 minutes for regular-sized cupcakes, or until the cupcakes are puffed and spring back when gently pressed in the middle. Cool the cupcakes in the tin until just warm, then tip them onto a cooling rack.

9. Cool completely before brushing with Fresh Lemon Double-Glaze.

Makes 20 mini or 8 regular-sized Fresh Lemon Cupcakes.

FRESH LEMON CUPCAKES WITH
FRESH LEMON DOUBLE-GLAZE (PAGE 102)

FRESH LEMON DOUBLE-GLAZE [GF]

Two coatings of this glaze give a tart twist to Fresh Lemon Cupcakes (see page 100).

SUPPLIES

sieve, measuring cups, bowl, reamer, ordinary teaspoon, measuring spoons, pastry brush

INGREDIENTS

4 tbsp icing sugar (spoon in, level; see page 19)

1 tbsp fresh lemon juice

1 drop yellow food colouring, if you like

PICTURED ON PAGE 101

1. Sift the icing sugar into a bowl.

2. Use a reamer to juice a lemon, scooping out the seeds with an ordinary teaspoon (throw away the seeds). Stir 1 tbsp of the juice into the icing sugar. Then stir in the food colouring, if using.

3. Dip your pastry brush into the glaze and paint it on top of the cupcakes. Let them dry a few minutes, then brush on a second coat. Let the glaze dry before eating.

Makes enough Fresh Lemon Double-Glaze for 20 mini or 8 regular-sized cupcakes.

102 EVERYDAY KITCHEN FOR KIDS } your own bakery

Sugared Doughnut Puffs

Mini muffins that taste like doughnuts! Shake them in a bag of cinnamon sugar for a genuine doughnut shop finish.

SUPPLIES

pastry brush, cling film, mini-muffin tin (up to 20 holes), liquid measuring cup, bowls, measuring cups, measuring spoons, fork or small whisk, baking spatula, dinner knife, ordinary teaspoon, paper lunch bag or plastic bag

INGREDIENTS

soft butter for muffin tin

125 ml milk

1 tbsp white sugar

1 tsp quick-rise yeast

250 ml (1 cup) plain flour (spoon in, level; see page 19)

⅛ tsp salt

1 tbsp unsalted butter

1 egg

½ tsp vanilla extract

⅛ tsp lemon extract, if you have it

1 tbsp plain flour

1 tbsp unsalted butter

2 tbsp white sugar

¼ tsp ground cinnamon, if you like

1. Use a pastry brush or a scrunched-up piece of cling film to generously butter 20 mini-muffin holes. Set aside.

2. In a microwave-safe liquid measuring cup, heat the milk in the microwave at 50% power for 1 minute (or longer) until very warm but not hot (see "Yeast," page 19). Sprinkle in the 1 tbsp sugar and the yeast. Do not stir. Cover with cling film and let stand for 10 minutes for the yeast to turn foamy.

3. In a large bowl, mix the flour and salt. Set aside.

4. In a small microwave-safe bowl, heat 1 tbsp butter in the microwave on 50% power until melted (about 30 seconds). Set aside.

CONTINUED ON NEXT PAGE

Sugared Doughnut Puffs (cont'd)

(5) Go back to the cup of foamy yeast. Use a fork or small whisk to beat in the egg. Next use a baking spatula to scrape the melted butter into the egg mixture. Add the vanilla and lemon extract, if using. Mix well with the fork or whisk.

(6) Using the baking spatula, scrape the wet mixture into the flour mixture. Stir into a stretchy dough batter. Scrape sticky ingredients off the spatula with a dinner knife so everything is well blended. When there is no dry flour left, cover the bowl with cling film. Let rise for 30 minutes in a warm spot.

(7) After the dough batter has risen, sprinkle the 1 tbsp flour onto it and stir it in until no more dry flour can be seen.

(8) Preheat the oven to 190°C/170°C fan/gas 5.

(9) Use an ordinary teaspoon to scoop spoonfuls of dough batter about the size of walnuts, and push them off the spoon with your finger into the 20 mini-muffin cups. Fill each cup about two-thirds full.

(10) Bake on the middle rack of the oven for 15 to 17 minutes, until lightly golden. Get help removing them from the oven.

(11) While the puffs are cooling, in a small microwave-safe bowl heat 1 tbsp butter in the microwave at 50% power until melted (about 30 seconds).

(12) With the puffs still in the tin, brush the tops with the melted butter. Take the puffs out of the tin.

(13) Put the 2 tbsp sugar and the cinnamon, if using, in a paper lunch bag or plastic bag. Drop in ten puffs. Close the bag tightly at the top and shake to coat the puffs in cinnamon sugar. Remove from the bag and shake the other ten puffs. Eat while warm.

Makes about 20 Sugared Doughnut Puffs.

Chocolate Banana Loaf

It's like magic: you can't see or taste the bananas, only the rich flavour of chocolate.

SUPPLIES

20 × 10 cm loaf tin, parchment paper, pastry brush or cling film, measuring spoons, bowls, sieve, measuring cups, baking spatula, wooden spoon, potato masher, dinner knife, toothpick

INGREDIENTS

soft butter for tin

375 ml (1½ cups) plain flour (spoon in, level; see page 19)

5 tbsp unsweetened cocoa powder (spoon in, level)

1 tsp baking soda

pinch of salt

4 tbsp chocolate chips, if you wish

160 ml (⅔ cup) white sugar

5 tbsp soft unsalted butter (see "Butter," page 16)

1 egg

2 ripe bananas

5 tbsp milk

1 tsp vanilla extract

1 tsp white vinegar

(1) Preheat the oven to 180°C/160°C fan/gas 4.

(2) Trace the bottom of a loaf tin on a piece of parchment paper. Cut out the rectangle a little smaller than your tracing. Check to see that the cutout can lie flat in the bottom of the tin and does not come up the sides. Use a pastry brush or a scrunched-up piece of cling film to rub butter on the bottom and sides of the loaf tin. Stick the cut-out parchment to the butter on the tin bottom. Set aside.

(3) Into a bowl, sift the flour, cocoa powder, baking soda, and salt. Mix well with a baking spatula. Stir in the chocolate chips, if using. Set aside.

CONTINUED ON NEXT PAGE

Chocolate Banana Loaf (cont'd)

(4) In another bowl, cream together the sugar and butter using the back of a wooden spoon. Mix in the egg. Set aside.

(5) Peel the bananas into a third bowl. Use a potato masher or the back of a wooden spoon to mash the bananas to a pulp. Stir the milk, vanilla, and vinegar into the bananas. Using a baking spatula, scrape the banana mixture into the butter mixture. Mix well.

(6) In two batches, stir the flour mixture into the wet mixture. Use a dinner knife to scrape sticky ingredients off the spatula. Stir just until no more dry flour can be seen.

(7) Using the baking spatula, scrape the batter into the prepared tin. Spread out evenly.

(8) Bake for 50 minutes, or until the top of the loaf has a crack along it and a toothpick inserted into the middle of the loaf comes out clean. Cool in the tin before getting help tipping out the loaf.

Makes 1 Chocolate Banana Loaf.

Warm Chocolate Brioches

Lovely little sweetened breads
filled with warm chocolate.

SUPPLIES

pastry brush or cling film, regular-
sized muffin tin (8 holes), measuring
cups, measuring spoons, bowls, cling
film, fork, baking spatula, dinner knife,
ordinary teaspoon

INGREDIENTS

soft butter for muffin tin

185 ml milk

2 tbsp unsalted butter

3 tbsp white sugar

1 tsp quick-rise yeast

2 eggs

2 egg yolks (see "Eggs," page 16)

½ tsp lemon extract

½ tsp vanilla extract

410 ml (1 ⅔ cups) plain flour (spoon in,
   level; see page 19)

½ tsp salt

125 ml (½ cup) plain flour (spoon in,
   level)

24 chocolate baking wafers

2 tbsp apricot jam

1. Using a pastry brush or a scrunched-up piece of cling film,
   butter eight muffin holes. Set aside.

2. Put the milk and butter in a large microwave-safe bowl. Heat
   in the microwave on high until the butter is melted (about
   30 seconds). Stir in the sugar. When the mixture is very warm
   but not hot (see "Yeast," page 19), sprinkle on the yeast, but
   do not stir again. Cover with cling film and set aside for
   10 minutes to let the yeast turn foamy.

3. After the yeast foams, use a fork to beat the eggs, egg yolks,
   lemon extract, and vanilla into the mixture. Set aside.

CONTINUED ON NEXT PAGE

Warm Chocolate Brioches (cont'd)

(4) In another large bowl, mix the 410 ml (1 ⅔ cups) flour and salt. Use a baking spatula to scrape the yeast mixture into the flour mixture. Mix into a very soft dough. Use a dinner knife to scrape sticky ingredients off the spatula so everything is well blended. Cover the bowl with cling film and let the dough rise for 30 minutes in a warm spot.

(5) Preheat the oven to 180°C/160°C fan/gas 4.

(6) When the dough has risen, uncover it and stir in 125 ml (½ cup) flour until no more dry flour can be seen. Scoop out about one-third of the dough into another bowl and set aside.

(7) Returning to the bowl with the larger amount of dough, use an ordinary teaspoon to scoop equal amounts into the eight buttered muffin holes.

(8) Next, stick chocolate wafers into the dough in the muffin tins. To do this, hold three chocolate wafers together in a stack on their side—the way you'd hold three coins together to drop into a slot in a piggy bank. Press the chocolate wafers into the middle of each hole of dough until they touch the bottom of the muffin hole. Push three wafers into each of the eight holes of dough.

(9) Now go to the bowl with the smaller amount of dough. Scoop spoonfuls of dough and use your finger to push it off the spoon and onto the tops of the muffin tin, completely covering the tops of the chocolate wafers.

(10) Bake on the middle rack of the oven for 25 minutes, or until lightly golden. Cool the brioches to lukewarm before removing them from the muffin tin.

(11) Put the apricot jam in a small microwave-safe bowl and heat in the microwave at 50% power until the jam is runny (about 30 seconds). Use the pastry brush to brush the jam onto the tops of the brioches until shiny. Enjoy the brioches while warm.

Makes 8 Warm Chocolate Brioches.

Little Fresh Blueberry Pies

SUPPLIES

sieve, measuring cups, measuring spoons, bowls, wooden spoon, dinner knife, four 12 cm pie tins (use the disposable foil type often sold for making little meat pies), baking spatula, baking sheet, ordinary teaspoon

INGREDIENTS

PIE SHELLS

160 ml (⅔ cup) plain flour (spoon in, level; see page 19)

2 tbsp icing sugar

¼ tsp baking soda

pinch of salt

4 tbsp soft unsalted butter (see "Butter," page 16)

1 tsp vegetable oil

½ tsp white vinegar

CREAM CHEESE LAYER

4 tbsp soft cream cheese (see "Cream Cheese," page 16)

4 tbsp icing sugar (spoon in, level)

½ tsp lemon juice

FRESH BLUEBERRY FILLING

5 tbsp grape jelly

250 ml (1 cup) fresh blueberries

Make your own pie shells! You bake them first, then load them with a sweet, creamy filling and fresh, juicy blueberries.

1. Preheat the oven to 180°C/160°C fan/gas 4.

2. To make the pie shells, sift the flour, icing sugar, baking soda, and salt into a bowl. Mix with a wooden spoon and set aside.

3. In another bowl, use the back of the wooden spoon to cream together the butter, vegetable oil, and vinegar. Add the flour mixture and stir to form a soft dough. Use a dinner knife to scrape sticky ingredients off the spoon. Use your hands to press the dough together to make the crumbly bits hold together. The dough should hold together when you pinch it. If it breaks apart, it is too dry and you should squeeze in another ⅛ tsp vegetable oil. This is the pastry for the pie shells.

4. Divide the pastry into two equal pieces. Use your fingers to press one piece into the bottom and up the sides of one pie tin. Make the thickness as even as possible. Check that the pastry is not too thick where it goes up the sides of the tin. Neaten the edges around the rim. Do the same with the second piece of pastry in a second tin.

5. Place the pastry-filled tins onto a baking sheet. Now take the two empty pie tins and place one onto each pie shell, pressing down gently (the empty tins don't need to slide all the way down to the bottom of the pastry). Leave the tins inside the pie shells during baking. They stop the pastry from puffing up too much as it bakes.

6. Bake the pie shells for 20 minutes. Remove them from the oven (keep the oven on) and cool them to lukewarm. Then gently lift out the empty pie tins. Return the pastry-filled pie tins to the oven to bake for another 5 minutes, or until the bottoms of the pie shells aren't moist anymore. You're now finished with the oven and can turn it off. Set aside the pie shells to cool to room temperature—do not take them out of the tins.

CONTINUED ON PAGE 111

LITTLE FRESH BLUEBERRY PIES

Little Fresh Blueberry Pies (cont'd)

⑦ While the pie shells cool, make the cream cheese filling. Put the cream cheese into a large bowl and mix it with a baking spatula or clean wooden spoon until it's very soft and creamy. Sift in the icing sugar, then add the lemon juice and mix until smooth. Set aside.

⑧ Next, make the glaze for the blueberries by placing the grape jelly in a large microwave-safe bowl and heating it in the microwave at 50% power until it's melted and runny. (Heat 30 seconds at a time; stir after each heating to check if it's runny. Heat two or three times.) Stir the melted jelly with a baking spatula until smooth. Cool to lukewarm. Stir the blueberries into the melted jelly until they are well coated. Set aside.

⑨ To assemble the pies, use an ordinary teaspoon to spread half the cream cheese mixture in the bottom of each pie shell. Then use a clean teaspoon to pile each pie with half the glazed blueberries. Chill the pies for at least 20 minutes before eating.

Makes 2 Little Fresh Blueberry Pies.

Pecan Sweetie Pies

SUPPLIES

sieve, measuring cups, measuring spoons, bowls, wooden spoon, dinner knife, two 12 cm pie tins (can use the disposable foil type often sold for making little meat pies), baking sheet, baking spatula, whisk

INGREDIENTS

PIE SHELLS

160 ml (⅔ cup) plain flour (spoon in, level; see page 19)

2 tbsp icing sugar

¼ tsp baking soda

pinch of salt

4 tbsp soft unsalted butter (see "Butter," page 16)

1 tsp vegetable oil

½ tsp white vinegar

FILLING

1 tbsp unsalted butter

125 ml (½ cup) firmly packed brown sugar

1 tbsp maple syrup

1 tbsp milk

¼ tsp vanilla extract

pinch of salt

1 egg

4 tbsp pecan pieces

Be patient with these small pies after they come out of the oven, because the buttery filling needs to cool to firm up before you can eat it.

(1) Preheat the oven to 180°C/160°C fan/gas 4.

(2) To make the pie shells, sift the flour, icing sugar, baking soda, and salt into a bowl. Mix with a wooden spoon and set aside.

(3) In another bowl, use the back of the wooden spoon to cream together the butter, vegetable oil, and vinegar. Add the flour mixture and stir to form a soft dough. Use a dinner knife to scrape the sticky bits off the spoon and use your hands to press any crumbly bits into the dough. The dough should hold together when you pinch it. If it breaks apart, it is too dry and you should squeeze in another ⅛ tsp vegetable oil. This is the pastry you will use to make the pie shells.

(4) Divide the pastry into two equal pieces. Use your fingers to press one piece into the bottom and up the sides of one pie tin. Make the thickness as even as possible. Check that the pastry is not too thick where it goes up the sides. Neaten the edges around the rim. Do the same with the second piece of pastry in the second tin.

(5) Place the pastry-filled pie tins onto a baking sheet.

(6) To make the filling, put the butter in a microwave-safe bowl and heat in the microwave at 50% power until melted (about 30 seconds). Use a baking spatula to stir in the brown sugar, maple syrup, milk, vanilla, and salt. Switch to a whisk to mix in the egg.

(7) Pour equal amounts of the filling into the two pie shells. Sprinkle equal amounts of the pecans on top of the filling. Do not stir.

(8) Get help putting the baking sheet and tins into the oven. Bake for 30 to 35 minutes, or until the filling puffs and the pastry edges are golden. Cool completely before eating.

Makes 2 Pecan Sweetie Pies.

PECAN SWEETIE PIES

Rainy Day Banana Bread

[GF]

SUPPLIES

20 × 10 cm loaf tin, parchment paper, pastry brush or cling film, bowls, whisk, measuring cups, measuring spoons, potato masher or wooden spoon, baking spatula, dinner knife, cooling rack

INGREDIENTS

soft butter for tin

160 ml (⅔ cup) brown rice flour (spoon in, level; see page 19)

160 ml (⅔ cup) white sugar

125 ml (½ cup) sorghum flour (spoon in, level)

125 ml (½ cup) tapioca flour (spoon in, level)

1 tsp xanthan gum

½ tsp baking powder

½ tsp salt

¼ tsp baking soda

¼ tsp ground cinnamon

4 tbsp unsalted butter

2 ripe bananas

2 eggs

2 tbsp plain yogurt

1 tsp vanilla extract

O.J. Glaze, if you like (see page 115)

It doesn't have to be raining to make this loaf, of course. It's good any time. Use ripe bananas for best flavour. If you prefer a non-gluten-free version, try the Chocolate Banana Loaf (page 105) or see the original *Kids Kitchen* cookbook for Banana Fudge Bread.

1. Preheat the oven to 180°C/160°C fan/gas 4.

2. Trace the bottom of the loaf tin on a piece of parchment paper. Cut the rectangle a little smaller than your tracing. Check that the cutout can lie flat in the bottom of the tin. Use a pastry brush or a scrunched-up piece of cling film to rub butter on the bottom and sides of the loaf tin. Stick the cut-out parchment to the butter on the tin bottom. Set aside.

3. In a large bowl, use a whisk to stir the 160 ml (⅔ cup) brown rice flour, sugar, sorghum flour, tapioca flour, xanthan gum, baking powder, salt, baking soda, and cinnamon. Whisk out any lumps. Set aside.

4. In a microwave-safe bowl, melt the 4 tbsp butter in the microwave at 50% power (about 1 minute). Set aside.

5. Peel the bananas into another large bowl. Use a potato masher or the back of a wooden spoon to mash the bananas to a pulp. Stir in the eggs, yogurt, and vanilla. Mix well.

6. Using a baking spatula, scrape the banana mixture and melted butter into the flour mixture. Stir until no dry flour is left. Use a dinner knife to scrape sticky ingredients off the spatula. Scrape the batter into the loaf tin. Spread evenly.

7. Bake on the middle rack of the oven 50 minutes, or until golden. Cool completely before getting help tipping out the bread. Peel off the parchment paper on the bottom. Set the loaf on a cooling rack to drizzle with O.J. Glaze, if you like.

Makes 1 loaf of Rainy Day Banana Bread.

O.J. GLAZE [GF]

A tangy orange juice glaze that tastes great drizzled on Rainy Day Banana Bread (see page 114).

SUPPLIES

sieve, measuring cup, bowl, measuring spoon, baking spatula, dinner knife, ordinary teaspoon

INGREDIENTS

250 ml (1 cup) icing sugar (spoon in, level; see page 19)

2 tbsp orange juice

Sift the icing sugar into a large bowl. Add the orange juice. Use a baking spatula to stir smooth. Scrape sticky ingredients from the spatula with a dinner knife.

Use an ordinary teaspoon to drizzle the glaze over the banana bread, letting the glaze dribble down the sides. Let stand a few minutes to harden.

Makes enough O.J. Glaze for 1 loaf of Rainy Day Banana Bread.

RAINY DAY BANANA BREAD WITH O.J. GLAZE

Blueberry Sunshine Muffins

[GF]

SUPPLIES

12 paper cupcake liners, 12-hole muffin tin, bowls, baking spatula, measuring cups, measuring spoons, wooden spoon, whisk, dinner knife, ordinary teaspoon

INGREDIENTS

160 ml (⅔ cup) sorghum flour (spoon in, level; see page 19)

125 ml (½ cup) brown rice flour (spoon in, level)

1½ tsp baking powder

½ tsp baking soda

½ tsp unflavoured gelatin powder

pinch of salt

160 ml (⅔ cup) white sugar

5 tbsp soft unsalted butter (see "Butter," page 16)

2 eggs

5 tbsp milk

½ tsp vanilla extract

125 ml (½ cup) fresh or frozen blueberries

Make a batch of these for a weekend breakfast! No speciality gluten-free gums are required. If you prefer a non-gluten-free version, see the original *Kids Kitchen* cookbook for Blueberry Muffins with Cinnamon Sugar.

1. Preheat the oven to 180°C/160°C fan/gas 4.

2. Place paper cupcake liners in 12 muffin holes.

3. In a bowl, using a baking spatula, mix the sorghum flour, brown rice flour, baking powder, baking soda, gelatin powder, and salt. Set aside.

4. In a second bowl—make this a big one—use the back of a wooden spoon to cream together the sugar and butter. Use a whisk to mix in the eggs, milk, and vanilla. Mix as smooth as you can, but don't worry if it's a little lumpy.

5. Now pour the flour mixture into the bowl of wet ingredients. Stir with the baking spatula just until no dry flour is left. Use a dinner knife to scrape sticky ingredients off the spatula so everything is well blended. This is the batter.

6. Continue using the baking spatula to gently stir the blueberries into the batter. Try not to squish the blueberries.

7. Use an ordinary teaspoon to scoop the batter into the 12 paper-lined muffin cups.

8. Bake the muffins for about 25 minutes, or until golden and the middle of a muffin springs back when gently pressed. Remove the muffins from the oven and cool in the tin until just warm.

Makes 12 Blueberry Sunshine Muffins.

BLUEBERRY SUNSHINE MUFFINS

APRICOT SCOOP CAKE

Apricot Scoop Cake

A moist vanilla cake made with lots of juicy fruit and no egg. You scoop the soft, warm cake to serve it, so there's no slicing.

SUPPLIES

pastry brush or cling film, 20 cm square glass or ceramic baking dish (or 8 × 23 cm baking dish), sieve, can opener, bowls, measuring cups, measuring spoons, wooden spoon, whisk, baking spatula

INGREDIENTS

soft butter for baking dish

1 can (400g) apricot halves or peach slices

250 ml (1 cup) plain flour (spoon in, level; see page 19)

1 tsp baking powder

⅛ tsp salt

250 ml (1 cup) white sugar

125 ml (½ cup) soft unsalted butter (see "Butter," page 16)

5 tbsp sour cream (5% milk fat or higher)

2 tbsp milk

1 tsp vanilla extract

eat with vanilla ice cream, if you like

1. Preheat the oven to 180°C/160°C fan/gas 4.

2. Using a pastry brush or a scrunched-up piece of cling film, butter the bottom and sides of the baking dish.

3. Set a large sieve over a big bowl. Open the canned apricots or peaches and pour into the sieve to drain. Set aside.

4. In another bowl and using a wooden spoon, mix the flour, baking powder, and salt. Set aside.

5. In a third large bowl, use the back of the wooden spoon to cream together the sugar, butter, and sour cream. Switch to a whisk to stir in the milk and vanilla until smooth. Gradually add the flour mixture and stir with the whisk until you have a thick batter.

6. Use a baking spatula to stir the drained fruit into the cake batter. Use the baking spatula to scrape the batter into the baking dish and spread it out evenly. Use a dinner knife to scrape off any batter stuck to the baking spatula into the dish. (Throw away the liquid drained from the can of fruit.)

7. Bake for 45 to 50 minutes, or until the cake is puffy and golden. Cool until just warm before eating. Scoop out the cake and serve with vanilla ice cream, if you like.

Serves up to 8 if eating with ice cream.

Little Black Forest Cake

SUPPLIES

15 to 17 cm diameter ceramic ramekin or soufflé dish, parchment paper, pastry brush or cling film, bowls, sieve, measuring cups, measuring spoons, wooden spoon, dinner knife, whisk, baking spatula, toothpick, work board, knife (for helper), plate

INGREDIENTS

CAKE

soft butter for baking dish

185 ml (¾ cup) plain flour (spoon in, level; see page 19)

4 tbsp unsweetened cocoa powder (spoon in, level)

1½ tsp baking powder

pinch of salt

5 tbsp soft unsalted butter (see "Butter," page 16)

160 ml (⅔ cup) white sugar

1 tsp vanilla extract

2 eggs

5 tbsp milk

FILLINGS AND TOPPINGS

125 ml (½ cup) cherry jam or pie filling

185 ml (¾ cup) whipped cream

½ tsp chocolate sprinkles, if you like

5 candied or maraschino cherries, if you like

If you have the right baking dish, you can make this little cake that can be cut into two layers. If you don't have the right dish, you can still make lots of other cakes in this book. (There's also an assortment of cakes in the original *Kids Kitchen* cookbook.)

1. Preheat the oven to 180°C/160°C fan/gas 4.

2. To prepare the cake dish, first trace the bottom of the ramekin or soufflé dish onto parchment paper. Cut out the parchment circle a little smaller than the tracing so it lies flat in the bottom of the dish. Make sure the cutout can lie flat in the bottom of the dish. Using a pastry brush or a scrunched-up piece of cling film, butter the bottom and sides of the dish. Press the circle of parchment paper in the bottom of the dish. The butter will hold the paper in place. Set aside.

3. In a large bowl, sift the plain flour, cocoa powder, baking powder, and salt. Mix with a wooden spoon and set aside.

4. In another large bowl, use the back of the wooden spoon to cream together the 5 tbsp butter, sugar, and vanilla. Use a dinner knife to scrape off any sticky ingredients on the spoon. Use a whisk to stir in about half the flour mixture. Then stir in the eggs. Finally, stir in the rest of the flour mixture and the milk. Stir with the whisk until smooth.

5. Use a baking spatula to scrape the batter into the cake dish. Use the dinner knife to clean off the spatula.

6. Bake for 35 to 40 minutes, or until a toothpick inserted in the middle comes out clean. Cool completely before getting help to tip the cake onto a work board. Peel off the parchment paper and get help cutting the cake in half horizontally.

(7) Set the bottom half of the cake on a plate and use a clean baking spatula to spread the cherry jam or pie filling on it. Then spread half the whipped cream over the jam.

(8) Place the top half of the cake on the whipped cream. Use a clean baking spatula to spread the rest of the whipped cream on the top of the cake, but not on the sides. Decorate with chocolate sprinkles and cherries, if you like.

Serves 4 (generously).

LITTLE BLACK FOREST CAKE

Pink Cherry Cake

SUPPLIES

20 cm round cake tin, parchment paper, pastry brush or cling film, kitchen scissors, bowls, measuring spoons, measuring cups, wooden spoon, dinner knife, whisk, baking spatula; if frosting: plate, parchment paper, baking spatula or palette knife

INGREDIENTS

soft butter for baking tin

8 candied or maraschino cherries

250 ml (1 cup) + 1 tbsp plain flour (spoon in, level; see page 19)

2 tsp baking powder

pinch of salt

185 ml (¾ cup) white sugar

5 tbsp soft unsalted butter (see "Butter," page 16)

1 egg

160 ml milk

1 tsp cherry extract

2 or 3 drops red food colouring

Pink Cloud Frosting, if you like (see page 124)

A moist, pink cake with cherries at the bottom.

1. Preheat the oven to 180°C/160°C fan/gas 4.

2. To prepare the cake tin, trace the bottom of the tin onto parchment paper. Cut out the paper circle a little smaller than the tracing so it lies flat in the bottom of the tin and doesn't bend up the sides. Use a pastry brush or a scrunched-up piece of cling film to butter the bottom and sides of the cake tin. Press the circle of parchment paper in the bottom of the tin. The butter will hold the paper in place. Set aside.

3. Use kitchen scissors to cut each cherry into about six small pieces. This job is fiddly, so be patient with it. Set aside the cherry pieces in a bowl.

4. In a big bowl, mix the flour, baking powder, and salt. Set aside.

5. In another large bowl, use the back of a wooden spoon to cream together the sugar and butter. Mix in the egg. Use a dinner knife to scrape sticky ingredients off the spoon. Use a whisk to stir in the milk and cherry extract until well mixed.

6. Use the whisk to gradually mix the flour mixture into the butter mixture. Stir in the food colouring to make the batter a nice shade of pink. Stir in the cherry pieces.

7. Use a baking spatula to scrape the batter into the cake tin. Use the dinner knife to scrape off sticky ingredients on the spatula. Bake 35 minutes, or until the middle of the cake springs back when gently pressed. Cool completely in the tin before getting help to tip out the cake. If you like, spread with Pink Cloud Frosting using a baking spatula or palette knife (see "Tips on Frosting Cakes," page 125). Keep the cake chilled until serving time.

Serves 8 to 10.

PINK CHERRY CAKE WITH

PINK CLOUD FROSTING (PAGE 124)

PINK CLOUD FROSTING

[GF]

Light as air and delightfully creamy, this is ideal for frosting Pink Cherry Cake (page 122) (or any 20 cm round cake or up to eight regular-sized cupcakes). Keep chilled any baked goods decorated with this frosting.

SUPPLIES

measuring cup, bowl, sieve, measuring spoon, baking spatula

INGREDIENTS

500 ml whipped cream

small pinch of salt

3 tbsp icing sugar

1 or 2 drops red or pink food colouring

1. Put the whipped cream and salt into a big bowl.

2. Sift the icing sugar onto the whipped cream. Use a baking spatula to fold the icing sugar into the whipped cream, then fold in the food colouring. Mix until the frosting is an even pink colour.

Makes enough Pink Cloud Frosting for one 20 cm round cake or 8 regular-sized cupcakes.

PICTURED ON PAGE 123

COCOA BUTTERCREAM FROSTING [GF]

Any kind of cream or milk will work in this recipe.

SUPPLIES

sieve, measuring cups, measuring spoons, bowls, baking spatula, wooden spoon, dinner knife

INGREDIENTS

500 ml (2 cups) icing sugar
  (spoon in, level; see page 19)

2 tbsp unsweetened
  cocoa powder

pinch of salt

2 tbsp soft unsalted butter
  (see "Butter," page 16)

5 tbsp cream (or milk)

1 tsp vanilla extract

1. Sift the icing sugar, cocoa powder, and salt into a big bowl. Mix well with a baking spatula. Set aside.

2. In another big bowl, use the back of a wooden spoon to cream the butter until it is very soft. Gradually stir in the icing sugar mixture and cream (or milk) until smooth. Mix in the vanilla. Use a dinner knife to scrape sticky ingredients off the wooden spoon so everything is well blended.

3. If you'd like the frosting to be creamier, stir in a spoonful more cream or milk. If it needs to be thicker, add a couple more spoons of sifted icing sugar.

Makes enough Cocoa Buttercream Frosting for one 20 cm round or square cake.

PICTURED ON PAGE 126

tips on frosting cakes

A cake is often made for a special occasion, so you'll want it to look as pretty as possible. Check out these tips to help make your cake look as good as it tastes!

HOW TO FROST A CAKE WITHOUT SMEARING THE PLATE

1. Use a plate a little bigger than the cake. Cut four 8 cm wide strips of parchment paper that are longer than the width of the plate (see photo, Surprising Chocolate Cake, on page 126). Overlap the strips so they form a square on the edges of the plate, even for round cakes.

2. You'll need a helper to tip the cake out of the baking tin and peel off the parchment from the bottom of the cake. Place the cake onto the strips of parchment so that the edges of the cake are on top of the parchment, not touching the plate.

3. Frost the top and sides of the cake using a baking spatula or palette knife. Add cake decorations, if any.

4. Pull out the strips of parchment from under the cake. You'll have a beautifully frosted cake on a perfectly clean plate!

   If you don't want to use the parchment strips, you can frost the cake without them, but be very careful when spreading the frosting onto the sides of the cake. After you finish frosting, carefully wipe the edges of the plate clean with the corner of a damp tea towel.

HOW TO AVOID CAKE CRUMBS IN THE FROSTING

As you spread frosting on a cake, pesky crumbs will get into the frosting. While you probably won't be able to avoid them all, there are a few things you can do to prevent crumbs from showing.

1. After you get your cake onto the cake plate, pick off any loose crumbs from the surface before you begin frosting.

2. Put one big blob of frosting onto the top of the cake and push it over the top and down the sides of the cake with your baking spatula or palette knife. Spreading one blob of frosting is better than spreading little bits of frosting at a time because that will cause cake crumbs to roll up.

DARK CAKES WITH LIGHT FROSTING

It can be especially tricky to frost a darker cake with a light-coloured frosting. If this is what you are trying to do, try this trick of frosting a cake twice to hide crumbs:

1. Use about half your frosting to spread a thin layer of frosting all over the cake. Don't worry at this point if crumbs get stuck in the frosting, this is just the bottom layer.

2. Chill the cake for 20 minutes or so. The crumbs will get "trapped" in the chilled frosting.

3. Finish by spreading the rest of your frosting on top of the chilled frosting layer. The crumbs are stuck in the bottom layer of frosting so they won't show in the top layer!

SURPRISING CHOCOLATE CAKE WITH

COCOA BUTTERCREAM FROSTING (PAGE 124)

Surprising Chocolate Cake

SUPPLIES

20 cm square glass or metal baking tin, parchment paper, pastry brush or cling film, bowls, sieve, measuring cups, measuring spoons, whisk, baking spatula, dinner knife; if frosting: plate, parchment paper, baking spatula or palette knife

INGREDIENTS

soft butter for baking dish

125 ml (½ cup) plain flour (spoon in, level; see page 19)

125 ml (½ cup) unsweetened cocoa powder (spoon in, level)

½ tsp baking powder

½ tsp baking soda

125 ml (½ cup) whole wheat flour (spoon in, level)

2 large eggs

185 ml (¾ cup) firmly packed brown sugar

125 ml (½ cup) unsweetened apple sauce

125 ml plain yogurt (not fat-free; the higher the milk fat, the moister the cake)

2 tsp vanilla extract

Cocoa Buttercream Frosting, if you like (see page 124)

A moist cake so chocolaty, you can't even taste the yogurt or apple sauce in it.

1. Preheat the oven to 180°C/160°C fan/gas 4.

2. To prepare the baking tin, trace the bottom of the tin on a piece of parchment paper. Cut out the square of parchment a little smaller than the shape you traced. Make sure the square of parchment can lie flat in the bottom of the baking tin and isn't too big that it bends up the sides. Use a pastry brush or a scrunched-up piece of cling film to butter the bottom and sides of the baking tin. Press the square of parchment paper in the bottom of the baking tin. The butter will hold the paper in place. Set aside.

3. In a bowl, sift in the plain flour, cocoa powder, baking powder, and baking soda. Use a whisk to stir in the whole wheat flour. Set aside.

4. In another bowl—a big one—use the whisk to mix the eggs, brown sugar, apple sauce, yogurt, and vanilla until smooth. Set aside.

5. Gradually add the flour mixture to the egg mixture. Use the whisk to stir the batter until no big lumps or dry flour are left.

6. Use a baking spatula to scrape the batter into the baking tin. Spread the batter evenly. Use a dinner knife to scrape off any sticky ingredients from the baking spatula into the tin.

7. Bake for 30 to 35 minutes, or until the middle of the cake springs back when gently pressed. Cool completely before getting help to tip out the cake. Use a baking spatula or palette knife to spread with Cocoa Buttercream Frosting, if you like (see "Tips on Frosting Cakes," page 125). Or you can keep the cake in the tin, spread frosting only on the top and slice pieces of cake out of the tin. To use up any leftover frosting, see Frosting Fudge, page 131.

Serves up to 12.

Vanilla Velvet Cake

[GF]

SUPPLIES

20 cm round cake tin, parchment paper, pastry brush or cling film, bowls, sieve, measuring cups, measuring spoons, baking spatula, wooden spoon, dinner knife, ordinary teaspoon, toothpick; if frosting: plate, parchment paper, baking spatula or palette knife

INGREDIENTS

soft butter for cake tin

250 ml (1 cup) white rice flour
  (glutinous; see "Rice Flour," page 18)
  (spoon in, level; see page 19)

4 tbsp potato starch (spoon in, level)

4 tbsp tapioca starch (spoon in, level)

1 tsp baking powder

1 tsp xanthan gum

¼ tsp salt

125 ml (½ cup) ricotta cheese

4 tbsp soft unsalted butter (see
  "Butter," page 16)

250 ml (1 cup) white sugar

2 eggs

2 tsp vanilla extract

4 tbsp milk

Vanilla Cream Frosting (see page 130)
  (or other frosting), if you like

sprinkles, if you wish

This simple but perfect treat tastes almost like pound cake. (See *Kids Kitchen* for a plain flour version—Classic Little Vanilla Cake.)

1. Preheat the oven to 180°C/160°C fan/gas 4.

2. To prepare the cake tin, trace the bottom of the tin onto parchment paper. Cut out the paper circle a little smaller than the tracing. Check to see that the cutout lies flat in the bottom of the tin and does not come up the sides. Use a pastry brush or a scrunched-up piece of cling film to butter the bottom and sides of the tin. Press the circle of parchment paper in the bottom of the tin. The butter will hold the paper in place. Set aside.

3. In a big bowl, sift the rice flour, potato starch, tapioca starch, baking powder, xanthan gum, and salt. Mix with a baking spatula and set aside.

4. In another big bowl, use the back of a wooden spoon to cream together the ricotta cheese and butter. Then cream in the sugar. Mix in the eggs and vanilla.

5. Gradually stir the flour mixture into the ricotta mixture until blended, then mix in the milk. Use a dinner knife to scrape sticky ingredients off the wooden spoon. You will have a stiff batter.

6. Use a baking spatula to scrape the batter into the cake tin, spreading evenly. The stiff batter might be bumpy on top. To smooth it out, dip an ordinary teaspoon in cold water and use the back of it to gently smooth out the bumps.

7. Bake for 38 to 40 minutes, or until the top of the cake is golden and a toothpick inserted into the middle comes out clean. Cool the cake in the tin before getting help taking the cake out of the tin. Use a baking spatula or palette knife to spread the cooled cake with frosting and add sprinkles, if you like (see "Tips on Frosting Cakes," page 125).

Serves up to 10.

VANILLA VELVET CAKE WITH
VANILLA CREAM FROSTING (PAGE 130)

VANILLA CREAM FROSTING [GF]

A smooth vanilla frosting you can use plain or tint with food colouring.

SUPPLIES

sieve, measuring cups, bowls, wooden spoon, whisk, ordinary teaspoon, measuring spoons, baking spatula

INGREDIENTS

875 ml (3 ½ cups) icing sugar (spoon
  in, level; see page 19)
5 tbsp sour cream (5% milk
  fat or more)
4 tbsp soft unsalted butter
  (see "Butter," page 16)
½ tsp lemon juice
½ tsp vanilla extract
small pinch of salt

1. Sift the icing sugar into a large bowl. Set aside.

2. In another large bowl, use a wooden spoon to roughly mash together the sour cream and butter. Switch to a whisk and stir in a couple heaped ordinary teaspoonfuls of the sifted icing sugar. Keep stirring hard. Be patient. At first the butter will stay in lumps but it will eventually blend into the icing sugar.

3. Stir in the lemon juice, vanilla, salt, and the rest of the icing sugar a few spoonfuls at a time. Mix until smooth. If the frosting is too thick, mix in another spoonful of sour cream. If it's too thin, stir in a couple more spoonfuls of sifted icing sugar.

Makes enough frosting for one 20 cm round or square cake.

PICTURED ON PAGE 129

FUDGY FROSTING [GF]

This will make enough frosting to cover any 20 cm round or square cake. As a bonus, you might have enough left over to make a little Frosting Fudge (page 131).

SUPPLIES

measuring cups, bowls, wooden spoon, measuring spoons

INGREDIENTS

250 ml (1 cup) semi-sweet chocolate
  chips
5 tbsp sour cream
¼ tsp vanilla extract
small pinch of salt

1. Put the chocolate chips in a microwave-safe bowl. Heat in the microwave at 50% power for 1½ minutes. Stir with a wooden spoon, then heat again at 50% power until melted (about 1 to 2 minutes, checking and stirring at 30-second intervals).

2. Get help removing the hot bowl from the microwave. Stir until the chocolate is smooth. Mix in the sour cream, vanilla, and salt until smooth.

PICTURED ON PAGE 132

Frosting Fudge

[GF]

This turns a bit of leftover frosting into a few bites of yummy fudge (the fudge shown is made from Fudgy Frosting, but you could also use leftover Cocoa Buttercream Frosting or Vanilla Cream Frosting).

If you would like to make larger batches of fudge, see the original *Kids Kitchen* cookbook for Classic Chocolate Fudge and Maple Nut Fudge.

SUPPLIES

measuring cups, measuring spoons, sieve, bowl, baking spatula, cling film, dinner knife

INGREDIENTS

leftover frosting (see pages 124 and 130)

icing sugar

few drops milk

spoonful walnut or pecan pieces, if you like

1. Measure how much frosting you have left over from icing a cake. For every 4 tbsp of frosting you have, you'll need up to 4 tbsp sifted icing sugar (when measuring, spoon in and level; see page 19). Mix together with a baking spatula. Use a dinner knife to scrape sticky ingredients off the spatula.

2. The fudge should be soft but not sticky. If the fudge is too soft, mix in another spoonful or two of sifted icing sugar. If the fudge is too stiff, mix in a few drops of milk. You can also mix in a spoonful of walnut or pecan pieces.

3. Scoop the fudge onto cling film. Cover with the wrap. Press the fudge into a 2.5 cm thick slab. Wrap tightly in the plastic and chill to firm up. Cut into cubes with a clean dinner knife before eating.

Makes 1 batch of Frosting Fudge.

DARK CHOCOLATE CAKE WITH
FUDGY FROSTING (PAGE 130)

Dark Chocolate Cake

[GF]

SUPPLIES

20 cm round cake tin, parchment paper, pastry brush or cling film, bowls, sieve, measuring cups for dry and liquid ingredients, measuring spoons, baking spatula, wooden spoon, toothpick; if frosting: plate, parchment paper, baking spatula or palette knife

INGREDIENTS

soft butter for cake tin

125 ml (½ cup) white rice flour (glutinous; see "Rice Flour," page 18) (spoon in, level; see page 19)

5 tbsp sorghum flour (spoon in, level)

5 tbsp tapioca starch (spoon in, level)

5 tbsp unsweetened cocoa powder (spoon in, level)

1 tsp baking powder

½ tsp xanthan gum

¼ tsp baking soda

pinch of salt

185 ml (¾ cup) white sugar

125 ml (½ cup) soft unsalted butter (see "Butter," page 16)

1 tbsp vanilla extract

3 eggs

5 tbsp milk

Fudgy Frosting, if you like (see page 130)

18 white chocolate baking wafers, if you like

A blend of flours makes this cake incredibly good. (See *Kids Kitchen* for an all-purpose-flour version—Easiest Chocolate Cake.)

1. Preheat the oven to 180°C/160°C fan/gas 4.

2. To prepare the cake tin, trace the bottom of the tin onto parchment paper. Cut the paper circle a little smaller than the tracing. Check to see that the cutout can lie flat in the bottom of the tin. Use a pastry brush or a scrunched-up piece of cling film to butter the bottom and sides of the cake tin. Press the circle of parchment in the bottom of the tin. The butter will hold the paper in place. Set aside.

3. Into a big bowl, sift the rice flour, sorghum flour, tapioca starch, cocoa powder, baking powder, xanthan gum, baking soda, and salt. Mix well with a baking spatula and set aside.

4. In another large bowl, use a wooden spoon to cream together the sugar, butter, and vanilla until smooth. Stir in the eggs and milk. Don't worry if the ingredients aren't fully mixed in.

5. Gradually stir the flour mixture into the egg mixture. Use the side of the baking spatula to mash out bigger lumps of butter. Stir the batter as smooth as you can. Scrape sticky ingredients off the spatula with a dinner knife. Don't worry if small bits of butter are left in the batter.

6. Use the baking spatula to scrape the batter into the tin. Clean off the spatula with the dinner knife.

7. Bake on the middle rack of the oven for 30 to 35 minutes, or until a toothpick stuck into the middle of the cake comes out clean. Cool completely in the tin before getting help taking the cake out of the tin. Spread with Fudgy Frosting and dot the top with white chocolate baking wafers, if you like (see "Tips on Frosting Cakes," page 125).

Serves up to 10.

Feta Focaccia Bread

SUPPLIES

measuring spoons, drinking cup, cling film, measuring cups, bowl, baking spatula, dinner knife, baking sheet, parchment paper, pastry brush

INGREDIENTS

BREAD

1 tsp white sugar

1 tsp quick-rise yeast

250 ml very warm (but not hot) water (see "Yeast," page 19)

500 ml (2 cups) plain flour (spoon in, level; see page 19)

½ tsp garlic powder

½ tsp dried oregano

¼ tsp salt

2 tbsp olive or vegetable oil

1 tbsp plain flour

TOPPINGS

2 tbsp crumbled feta cheese

1 tbsp Parmesan cheese

1 tbsp sliced black olives, if you like

½ tsp dried parsley

Golden and flecked with cheeses and herbs, this chewy bread looks and tastes like one you'd get from an Italian bakery.

1. Put the sugar and yeast in a drinking cup. Add the warm water. Do not stir. Cover with cling film and set aside to stand for 10 minutes to let the yeast turn foamy.

2. In a large bowl, using a baking spatula, mix the flour, garlic powder, dried oregano, and salt. Scrape in the foamy yeast mixture and 1 tbsp oil (the other tablespoon of oil is for later). Stir well. Use a dinner knife to scrape sticky ingredients off the spatula. Cover the bowl with cling film and let the dough rise for 30 minutes in a warm spot.

3. Line a baking sheet with parchment paper.

4. After the dough has risen, sprinkle 1 tbsp flour onto it. Then flour your hands and squeeze the tablespoon of flour into the dough. It will be very stretchy and loose. Tip the dough out of the bowl onto the parchment-lined baking sheet. Press the dough into a 2 cm thick slab—it doesn't matter what shape you make it.

5. Use a pastry brush to brush the dough with the remaining 1 tbsp oil. Let the dough rise another 30 minutes in a warm spot, uncovered.

6. Preheat the oven to 190°C/170°C fan/gas 5.

7. After the dough has risen again, use your pointer finger to poke down into the dough every 5 cm or so. When making your pokes, don't be afraid to push all the way down until your finger can feel the baking sheet underneath. The dough should look puffy and dotted with little dimples all over it.

8. Sprinkle on the cheeses, olives (if using), and dried parsley.

9. Bake on the middle rack of the oven for 25 minutes, or until the bread is golden.

Makes 1 loaf of Feta Focaccia Bread.

FETA FOCACCIA BREAD

Champion Ciabatta

SUPPLIES

liquid measuring cup, drinking cup, measuring spoons, cling film, baking sheet, parchment paper, bowls, baking spatula, measuring cups, fork, dinner knife, pastry brush

INGREDIENTS

160 ml very warm (but not hot) water (see "Yeast," page 19)

1½ tsp white sugar

½ tsp quick-rise yeast

375 ml (1½ cups) plain flour (spoon in, level; see page 19)

½ tsp salt

1 egg white (see "Eggs," page 16)

1 tbsp vegetable oil

4 tbsp plain flour (spoon in, level)

4 tbsp plain flour (spoon in, level)

2 tsp water

When you pull this delicious crusty bread out of the oven, you won't believe your eyes! You need to wait for the dough to rise a few times—but it's worth it!

1. Measure the warm water into a drinking cup. Sprinkle in the sugar and yeast. Do not stir. Cover with cling film and set aside for 10 minutes to let the yeast turn foamy.

2. Line a baking sheet with parchment paper.

3. In a big bowl and using a baking spatula, mix the plain flour and salt. Set aside.

4. Go back to the foamy yeast. Use a fork to beat in the egg white and vegetable oil. Use a baking spatula to scrape mixture into the flour mixture. Stir into a sticky batter. Use a dinner knife to scrape sticky ingredients off the spatula. Cover the bowl with cling film and let it stand for 30 minutes in a warm spot.

5. After the batter has finished rising, sprinkle one of the 4 tbsp flour over the batter. Use the baking spatula to stir until you don't see any more dry flour. The batter will turn into a soft dough. When it becomes too stiff to stir, use your hands to squeeze the dry flour into the dough. Cover the bowl again and let the dough rise for 15 minutes in a warm spot.

6. After this rising, sprinkle the second 4 tbsp flour onto the dough and squeeze it into the dough until you don't see any more dry flour. Cover the bowl and let the dough rise (last long rising!) for another 15 minutes in a warm spot.

7. After this rising, uncover the bowl, tip it on its side, flour your hands, and use your fingers to gently roll the dough out of the bowl and onto the middle of the parchment-lined baking sheet. Try not to squish the air out of the dough. Dust your hands with flour again and gently pat the sides of the blob of dough to make it into a long, oval shape, about 25 cm long and 8 cm wide.

8. Preheat the oven to 190°C/170°C fan/gas 5. As the oven heats, the bread (uncovered) will rise a bit more.

9. Use a pastry brush to gently brush 2 tsp water over the dough. Don't press down hard or you might squish the air out of the dough. The water helps make the bread crusty.

10. Bake on the middle rack of the oven for 30 minutes, or until golden. Eat while warm.

Makes 1 loaf of Champion Ciabatta.

Whole Wheat Sandwich Bread

SUPPLIES

20 × 10 cm loaf tin, parchment paper, pastry brush or cling film, bowls, measuring cups, measuring spoons, wooden spoon, baking spatula, whisk, dinner knife, knife (for helper)

INGREDIENTS

soft butter for loaf tin

250 ml milk

1 tsp white sugar

1 tsp quick-rise yeast

375 ml (1½ cups) whole wheat flour (spoon in, level; see page 19)

125 ml (½ cup) plain flour (spoon in, level)

½ tsp salt

2 tbsp unsalted butter

1 egg

125 ml (½ cup) plain flour (spoon in, level)

Sure, you could buy brown bread at the store, but it won't beat this one you make yourself!

① Trace the bottom of the loaf tin on a piece of parchment paper. Cut out the rectangle a little smaller than your tracing. Check to see that the cutout can lie flat in the bottom of the tin and does not come up the sides. Use a pastry brush or a scrunched-up piece of cling film to rub butter on the bottom and sides of the loaf tin. Stick the cut-out parchment to the butter on the tin bottom. Set aside.

② In a big microwave-safe bowl, heat the milk in the microwave at 50% power until it's very warm, but not hot (see "Yeast," page 19). This might take more than 1 minute, but heat only 1 minute at a time or the milk could foam over. Use a wooden spoon to stir in the sugar. Sprinkle in the yeast, but do not stir. Cover with cling film and set aside for 10 minutes to let the yeast turn foamy.

③ Meanwhile, in another large bowl, use a baking spatula to mix the 375 ml (1½ cups) whole wheat flour, 125 ml (½ cup) plain flour, and salt. Set aside.

④ You'll need another microwave-safe bowl to heat the butter in the microwave at 50% power until melted (about 30 seconds). Set aside. You have several bowls of ingredients now, but be patient; you're almost ready to mix them into a dough.

⑤ Go back to the milk and yeast mixture. Crack in the egg and use a whisk to mix until smooth. Use a baking spatula to scrape in the melted butter. Switch to the whisk to mix well.

⑥ Pour the wet mixture into the flour mixture. Scrape the wet bowl clean with the baking spatula, then use the spatula to stir the ingredients into a soft, smooth dough. Use a dinner knife to scrape off the spatula. Cover the bowl with cling film. Let the dough rise for 30 minutes in a warm spot.

(7) After the dough finishes rising, sprinkle on 125 ml (½ cup) plain flour. Use the baking spatula to mix until all the dry flour is gone. Scrape the dough into the loaf tin. Scrape the sticky ingredients off the spatula into the dough with the dinner knife. Let the dough rise, uncovered, for another 20 minutes in a warm spot.

(8) Preheat the oven to 180°C/160°C fan/gas 4 while the dough is rising.

(9) Bake on the middle rack of the oven for 40 to 45 minutes, until the bread is golden. Cool in the tin until lukewarm before tipping out. Peel off the parchment before getting help cutting the bread into slices.

Makes 1 loaf of Whole Wheat Sandwich Bread.

WHOLE WHEAT SANDWICH BREAD

Cheddar Egg Bread

SUPPLIES

20 × 10 cm loaf tin, parchment paper, pastry brush or cling film, bowls, measuring cups, measuring spoons, baking spatula, whisk, cling film, wooden spoon, dinner knife, knife (for helper)

INGREDIENTS

soft butter for loaf tin

185 ml milk

1 tbsp white sugar

1 tsp quick-rise yeast

2 tbsp unsalted butter

410 ml (1 ⅔ cups) plain flour (spoon in, level; see page 19)

5 tbsp pre-grated cheddar cheese

½ tsp salt

2 eggs

2 tbsp plain flour

Enjoy this yeast bread fresh or toasted, or for sandwiches. If you prefer a quicker version without rising times, see the original *Kids Kitchen* cookbook for the Cheddar Bread recipe.

1. Trace the bottom of the loaf tin on a piece of parchment paper. Cut out the rectangle a little smaller than your tracing. Check to see that the cutout can lie flat at the bottom of the tin and does not come up the sides. Use a pastry brush or a scrunched-up piece of cling film to rub butter on the bottom and sides of the loaf tin. Stick the cut-out parchment to the butter on the tin bottom. Set aside.

2. In a big microwave-safe bowl, heat the milk in the microwave at 50% power until it's very warm, but not hot (see "Yeast," page 19). This may take more than 1 minute, but heat only 1 minute at a time or the milk could foam over. Use a baking spatula to stir in the sugar. Sprinkle in the yeast, but do not stir. Cover with cling film and set aside for 10 minutes to let the yeast turn foamy.

3. Meanwhile, in another microwave-safe bowl, melt the butter in the microwave at 50% power (about 30 seconds). Set aside.

4. In another bowl, use a wooden spoon to mix the plain flour, cheese, and salt. Set aside.

5. Go back to the foamy yeast mixture. Use a whisk to mix in the eggs. Use the baking spatula to scrape in the butter. Switch to the whisk to mix well.

6. Pour the flour mixture into the wet mixture. Use the baking spatula to stir the ingredients into a soft, smooth dough. Be sure to mix in all the dry flour in the bottom of the bowl. Use a dinner knife to scrape off sticky ingredients on the spatula. Cover the bowl with cling film and set aside to rise for 30 minutes in a warm spot.

(7) When the dough has risen, use the baking spatula to stir in 2 tbsp plain flour. Mix until all the dry flour is gone. Scrape the dough into the loaf tin. Clean off the spatula with the dinner knife. Let the dough rise, uncovered, for another 20 minutes in a warm spot. The risings make the bread soft and delicious, so it's good to be patient.

(8) Preheat the oven to 180°C/160°C fan/gas 4 while the dough is rising.

(9) Bake for 30 to 35 minutes, until the bread is golden. Cool in the tin until lukewarm before tipping out. Peel off the parchment before getting help cutting the bread into slices.

Makes 1 loaf of Cheddar Egg Bread.

CHEDDAR EGG BREAD (LEFT) AND TOMATO SALSA CORNBREAD (PAGE 142)

Tomato Salsa Cornbread

SUPPLIES

SUPPLIES

20 × 10 cm loaf tin, parchment paper, pastry brush or cling film, bowls, measuring cups, ordinary teaspoon, baking spatula, measuring spoons, whisk, dinner knife, knife (for helper)

INGREDIENTS

soft butter for tin

5 tbsp milk

4 tbsp unsalted butter

185 ml (¾ cup) yellow cornmeal

185 ml (¾ cup) plain flour (spoon in, level; see page 19)

5 tbsp pre-grated cheddar cheese

1 tsp baking powder

1 tsp white sugar

½ tsp baking soda

½ tsp chilli powder

½ tsp dried oregano

½ tsp dried thyme

¼ tsp salt

2 eggs

5 tbsp tomato salsa (from jar or tub)

PICTURED ON PAGE 141

Jarred tomato salsa and dried herbs pack flavour into this moist cornbread. It's great for serving with stews, chicken, or ribs for dinner.

1. Preheat the oven to 190°C/170°C fan/gas 5.

2. Trace the bottom of the loaf tin onto a piece of parchment paper. Cut out the rectangle a little smaller than your tracing. Check that the cutout can lie flat in the bottom of the tin and does not come up the sides. Use a pastry brush or a scrunched-up piece of cling film to rub butter on the bottom and sides of the loaf tin. Stick the cut-out parchment to the butter on the tin bottom. Set aside.

3. In a big microwave-safe bowl, heat the milk and 4 tbsp butter in the microwave at 50% power until the butter is melted and the milk is warm (about 1 minute). Use an ordinary teaspoon to mix in the cornmeal to soak. Set aside.

4. In another bowl, use a baking spatula to mix the flour, cheese, baking powder, sugar, baking soda, chilli powder, oregano, thyme, and salt. Set aside.

5. Go back to the bowl of cornmeal mixture and use a whisk to mix in the eggs. Use the baking spatula to stir in the salsa. Pour the flour mixture to the cornmeal mixture. Stir with the spatula just until no more dry flour can be seen, but don't over-mix. Scrape this batter into the loaf tin. Use a dinner knife to clean sticky ingredients off the spatula.

6. Bake on the middle rack of the oven for 25 to 30 minutes, until the top of the cornbread is golden and it springs back when gently pressed in the middle. Cool in the tin until lukewarm before tipping out. Peel off the parchment before getting help cutting the bread into slices.

Makes 1 loaf of Tomato Salsa Cornbread.

Spring Onion Bread

PICTURED ON PAGE 145

SUPPLIES

20 × 10 cm loaf tin, parchment paper, pastry brush or cling film, measuring spoons, bowls, measuring cups, baking spatula, kitchen scissors, dinner knife, knife (for helper)

INGREDIENTS

soft butter for tin

4 tbsp unsalted butter

500 ml (2 cups) plain flour (spoon in, level; see page 19)

2 tsp baking powder

2 tsp white sugar

1 tsp onion powder

1 tsp salt

¼ tsp baking soda

2 spring onions

185 ml milk

125 ml (½ cup) ricotta cheese

2 eggs

1 tsp lemon juice

Fresh spring onions—also called scallions— snipped into the dough give this quick savoury bread a wonderful aroma as it bakes. Serve warm slices with lunch or dinner!

1. Preheat the oven to 180°C/160°C fan/gas 4.

2. Trace the bottom of the loaf tin on a piece of parchment paper. Cut out the rectangle a little smaller than your tracing. Check that the cutout can lie flat in the bottom of the tin and does not come up the sides. Use a pastry brush or a scrunched-up piece of cling film to rub butter on the bottom and sides of the loaf tin. Stick the cut-out parchment to the butter on the tin bottom. Set aside.

3. In a large microwave-safe bowl, heat the 4 tbsp butter in the microwave at 50% power until melted (about 1 minute). Set aside.

4. In another bowl, use a baking spatula to mix the flour, baking powder, sugar, onion powder, salt, and baking soda.

5. Use kitchen scissors to cut the spring onion into little pieces (about the size of your smallest fingernail) into the flour mixture (throw away or compost the root). Mix and set aside.

6. Go back to the bowl of butter. Use the baking spatula to stir in the milk and ricotta until well blended. Add the eggs and lemon juice and mix well.

7. Pour the flour mixture into the wet ingredients. Stir just until no more dry flour can be seen. Don't over-mix. Scrape the batter into the loaf tin, spreading evenly. Use a dinner knife to scrape the sticky ingredients off the spatula.

8. Bake for 45 to 50 minutes, until the bread is lightly browned and springs back when gently pressed in the middle. Cool in the tin until lukewarm before tipping out. Peel off the parchment before getting help cutting the bread into slices.

Makes 1 loaf of Spring Onion Bread.

Cheese Pizza Muffins

SUPPLIES

12 paper cupcake liners, 12-hole muffin tin, bowls, measuring cups, measuring spoons, baking spatula, whisk, dinner knife, ordinary teaspoon

INGREDIENTS

160 ml milk

4 tbsp unsalted butter

375 ml (1½ cups) plain flour (spoon in, level; see page 19)

2 tsp baking powder

1½ tsp dried Italian seasoning or oregano

1½ tsp white sugar

1 tsp chilli powder

½ tsp garlic salt

¼ tsp salt

¼ tsp baking soda

125 ml (½ cup) pre-grated cheddar cheese

2 eggs

5 tbsp tomato sauce

1 tbsp Parmesan cheese

These are not sweet muffins. Instead, they taste like cheese pizza. Enjoy them buttered like rolls or cut them open to make little sandwiches.

1. Preheat the oven to 180°C/160°C fan/gas 4.

2. Place paper cupcake liners in 12 muffin holes.

3. In a large microwave-safe bowl, heat the milk and butter in the microwave at 50% power until the butter is melted (about 1 minute). Set aside.

4. In another big bowl, use a baking spatula to mix the flour, baking powder, Italian seasoning or oregano, sugar, chilli powder, garlic salt, salt, baking soda, and cheddar cheese. Set aside.

5. Go back to the milk mixture. Pour it into the flour mixture.

6. Crack two eggs into the empty bowl that was used for the milk mixture. Use a whisk to mix the egg whites and yolks together. Pour the eggs into the bowl with the flour mixture. Use the baking spatula to mix until no more dry flour can be seen and the eggs are mixed in. Use a dinner knife to scrape sticky ingredients off the spatula. This is the batter.

7. Pour the tomato sauce onto the batter, but do not stir normally. Instead, use the baking spatula to stir only once or twice around the bowl. Just make streaks of tomato sauce in the batter. Don't mix it in completely.

8. Use an ordinary teaspoon to scoop up the batter. Push it off the spoon with your finger into the 12 lined holes. Fill the holes evenly.

9. Hold the tablespoon of Parmesan cheese over the cups of batter and lightly tap the side of the spoon so a sprinkling of cheese falls on top of the batter.

10. Bake for 25 to 27 minutes, until the muffins are golden. Cool to lukewarm in the tins before eating.

Makes 12 Cheese Pizza Muffins.

SPRING ONION BREAD (LEFT) (PAGE 143)
AND CHEESE PIZZA MUFFINS

your cookie jar

Bake a cookie for every
kind of craving!

CHOCOLATE CHIPPERS

Chocolate Chippers

SUPPLIES

2 baking sheets, parchment paper, bowls, baking spatula, measuring cups, measuring spoons, wooden spoon, ordinary teaspoon, dinner knife

INGREDIENTS

160 ml (⅔ cup) whole wheat flour (spoon in, level; see page 19)

2 tbsp plain flour

¼ tsp baking soda

⅛ tsp salt

4 tbsp soft unsalted butter (see "Butter," page 16)

4 tbsp firmly packed brown sugar

2 tbsp runny honey

1 egg yolk (see "Eggs," page 16)

1 tsp vanilla extract

5 tbsp chocolate chips

Honey-kissed whole wheat cookies with a little extra crunch!

1. Preheat the oven to 180°C/160°C fan/gas 4.

2. Line the baking sheets with parchment paper. (If you have only one baking sheet, after baking the first batch let the sheet cool before refilling it with the second batch of cookie dough.)

3. In a bowl and using a baking spatula, mix the whole wheat flour, plain flour, baking soda, and salt. Set aside.

4. In another large bowl, use the back of a wooden spoon to cream together the butter, brown sugar, and honey. Mix in the egg yolk and vanilla, but don't add the chocolate chips yet.

5. Using an ordinary teaspoon, gradually add spoonfuls of the flour mixture into the butter mixture. Stir with a wooden spoon until blended, using a dinner knife to scrape off sticky ingredients. Mix in the chocolate chips.

6. Use the teaspoon to scoop walnut-sized mounds of dough onto the parchment-lined baking sheets, pushing the dough off with your finger so the mounds are about 5 cm apart from each other. Make ten mounds on each sheet.

7. Bake on the middle rack of the oven, one sheet at a time, for 11 to 12 minutes, or until the cookies are lightly golden at the edges. Cool cookies at least 5 minutes on the sheets before eating.

Makes 20 Chocolate Chippers.

CLOCKWISE FROM LEFT: PEEK-A-POKES
(PAGE 153), CINNAMOONS, PEANUT BUTTER BEEZIES (PAGE 175)

Cinnamoons

SUPPLIES

2 baking sheets, parchment paper, bowls, sieve, measuring cups, measuring spoons, baking spatula, wooden spoon, dinner knife

INGREDIENTS

310 ml (1¼ cups) plain flour (spoon in, level; see page 19)

2 tsp ground cinnamon

½ tsp baking soda

½ tsp ground ginger

¼ tsp ground nutmeg

⅛ tsp salt

½ cup (125 ml) soft unsalted butter (see "Butter," page 16)

5 tbsp packed brown sugar

5 tbsp white sugar

4 tbsp molasses (any type you have)

1 egg yolk (see "Eggs," page 16)

½ tsp vanilla extract

2 tbsp unsweetened cocoa powder

Each bite is different because these cookies join together two kinds of dough: cinnamon-ginger and spicy cocoa.

1. Preheat the oven to 180°C/160°C fan/gas 4.

2. Line the baking sheets with parchment paper. (If you have only one baking sheet, this recipe will still work fine, but after baking the first batch you will need to let the sheet cool before refilling it with the second batch of cookie dough.)

3. Into a large bowl, sift the flour, cinnamon, baking soda, ginger, nutmeg, and salt. Mix well with a baking spatula.

4. In another large bowl, use a wooden spoon to cream together the butter and the brown and white sugars. Mix in the molasses, egg yolk, and vanilla. Do not add the cocoa powder yet.

5. To make the cinnamon-ginger dough, add half the flour mixture to all of the butter mixture and stir until most of the flour is blended in. Then stir in the rest of the flour mixture. Mix well. Use a dinner knife to scrape sticky ingredients from the wooden spoon.

6. For plain cinnamon-ginger cookies, you can use the dough (as it is now) and skip to step 9. But to make Cinnamoons, spoon out about half the dough into another bowl. Sift 2 tbsp cocoa powder into one of the bowls. Mix well into the dough. Now you will have one bowl of cinnamon-ginger dough and a second bowl with spicy cocoa dough.

7. Use a tablespoon to scoop into the cocoa dough; fill the spoon about halfway, then scoop the same half-filled spoon into the cinnamon-ginger dough and fill the spoon to the top (level, not mounded). Each cookie will have a slightly different-looking swirl of the two doughs.

CONTINUED ON NEXT PAGE

Cinnamoons (cont'd)

(8) Drop the dough—in one lump—onto the parchment-lined baking sheet, using your finger to gently pull the lump of dough out of the spoon; it's easiest if you pull at the edges and not the middle of the dough. Continue scooping the two kinds of dough into one spoon and dropping the mounds onto the parchment. Drop the mounds of dough 5 cm apart. Don't flatten the dough. The cookies spread as they bake.

(9) Fill up two baking sheets with 28 mounds of dough. Bake, one sheet at a time, on the middle rack of the oven for 11 to 12 minutes, or until the cookies have spread out, puffed up, and settled back down again. Cool on baking sheets until firm before eating.

Makes 28 Cinnamoons.

Peek-a-Pokes

SUPPLIES

2 baking sheets, parchment paper, kitchen scissors, measuring cups, bowls, baking spatula, measuring spoons, sieve, wooden spoon, dinner knife

INGREDIENTS

6 dried, pitted honey dates

160 ml (⅔ cup) + 2 tbsp whole wheat flour (spoon in, level; see page 19)

¼ tsp baking soda

pinch of salt

4 tbsp unsweetened cocoa powder (spoon in, level)

125 ml (½ cup) soft unsalted butter (see "Butter," page 16)

4 tbsp firmly packed brown sugar

4 tbsp white sugar

1 egg yolk (see "Eggs," page 16)

½ tsp vanilla extract

½ tsp white vinegar

PICTURED ON PAGE 150

Take a peek at these cookies with chewy bits of dates poking out all over.

1. Preheat the oven to 180°C/160°C fan/gas 4.

2. Line the baking sheets with parchment paper. (If you have only one baking sheet, this recipe will still work fine, but after baking the first batch you will need to let the sheet cool before refilling it with the second batch of cookie dough.)

3. Use kitchen scissors to cut the dates into little pieces the size of chocolate chips. Set aside.

4. In a bowl, use a baking spatula to mix the whole wheat flour, baking soda, and salt. Sift in the cocoa powder. Mix well. Set aside.

5. In another large bowl, use the back of a wooden spoon to cream together the butter and the brown and white sugars. Mix in the egg yolk, vanilla, and white vinegar until smooth.

6. Pour the flour mixture into the butter mixture. Stir with a baking spatula into a soft dough. Use a dinner knife to scrape sticky ingredients off the spatula. When the dough gets too hard to mix, use your hands to press it together, working in the crumbly bits in the bottom of the bowl. The dough is properly mixed when it is an even colour.

7. Sprinkle in the cut-up dates. Squeeze them in evenly through the dough.

8. Use a tablespoon to scoop eight mounds of dough onto each baking sheet. Push the dough off the spoon with your finger so the mounds are at least 5 cm apart. Don't flatten the dough.

9. Bake, one sheet at a time, on the middle rack of the oven for 13 to 15 minutes, until cookies have spread out and are no longer shiny on top. Cool until lukewarm before removing the cookies from the baking sheets.

Makes 16 Peek-a-Pokes

Old-Fashioned Sugar Cookies

SUPPLIES

bowl, wooden spoon, measuring cups, measuring spoons, cling film, 2 baking sheets, parchment paper, dinner knife, work board, rolling pin, cookie cutters

INGREDIENTS

160 ml (⅔ cup) white sugar

5 tbsp soft unsalted butter (see "Butter," page 16)

1 egg

½ tsp vanilla extract

pinch of salt

375 ml (1½ cups) plain flour (spoon in, level; see page 19)

Glossy Cookie Glaze, if you like

sprinkles, if you like

A handy recipe for making a small, perfect batch of dough for cookie cutters. Eat the cookies plain or decorate them with Glossy Cookie Glaze (see page 156).

1. In a large bowl, use the back of a wooden spoon to cream together the sugar and butter until well blended. Mix in the egg, vanilla, and salt until the mixture is smooth and no lumps of butter or unmixed egg are left.

2. Scoop two or three heaped spoonfuls of flour at a time into the butter mixture. Mix in as you add spoonfuls of flour. Keep adding flour and stirring it into the dough until all the flour is gone. When the dough gets too stiff to stir, use your hands to squeeze the rest of the flour into the butter mixture. Make sure the ingredients are mixed in evenly. You will end up with a soft dough.

3. Pat the dough into one big patty and leave it in the bowl. Cover it with cling film and chill in the fridge for 30 minutes.

4. After chilling the dough, preheat the oven to 170°C/150°C fan/ gas 3.

5. Line the baking sheets with parchment paper. (If you have only one baking sheet, this recipe will still work fine, but after baking the first batch you will need to let the sheet cool before refilling it with the second batch of cookie dough.) Also cut two other large pieces of parchment paper.

6. Use a dinner knife to cut the dough into two pieces.

7. On your work board, place a piece of dough between the two large pieces of parchment paper you cut in step 5. Place your rolling pin over the top sheet to roll out the dough to 5 mm thick (see "Two-Stacked-Pound-Coins Rule," page 19).

8. Peel off the top sheet of parchment. Cut the rolled dough with cookie cutters. Use the dinner knife to lift the cutouts off the board and lay them on the lined baking sheets 2.5 cm apart. Re-roll the dough scraps to cut again.

CONTINUED ON PAGE 156

OLD-FASHIONED SUGAR COOKIES WITH
GLOSSY COOKIE GLAZE (PAGE 156)

Old-Fashioned Sugar Cookies (cont'd)

9   When you are finished with the first piece of dough, roll and cut the second piece. If the cutouts get too soft to lift up, chill the dough again for about 10 minutes.

10   Bake, one sheet at a time, on the middle rack of the oven for 11 to 12 minutes, or until the edges of the cookies are lightly golden. Remove from the oven and let the cookies cool on the baking sheets before decorating with Glossy Cookie Glaze and sprinkles, if using.

Makes about 24 cookies, depending on the size of your cutters.

SUPPLIES

sieve, measuring cup, bowl, baking spatula, measuring spoons, small dishes, small, clean paintbrush or ordinary teaspoon

INGREDIENTS

330 ml (1⅓ cups) icing sugar (spoon in, level; see page 19)

1 tbsp lemon juice

1 tbsp milk

food colourings

GLOSSY COOKIE GLAZE [GF]

Brush or spoon this glaze onto any baked, rolled cookies such as Old-Fashioned Sugar Cookies (page 154) or Sugar Delights (page 170). The glaze hardens into a glossy coating after a few minutes at room temperature.

1   Sift the icing sugar into a bowl. Using a baking spatula, stir in the lemon juice and milk until smooth. The glaze should be the thickness of white glue. Sift and mix in a spoonful more icing sugar to thicken or a few more drops of milk if the glaze is too thick to spread.

2   To tint the glaze different colours, spoon out portions into small dishes and stir a drop of food colouring into each dish.

3   With a small, clean paintbrush or ordinary teaspoon, spread glaze on the cookies, using a clean brush or spoon for each colour. Leave the glazed cookies to dry.

Makes enough to glaze about 24 cookies.

Sweet Date Pockets

SUPPLIES

baking sheet, parchment paper, kitchen scissors, bowl, wooden spoon, measuring cups, measuring spoons, dinner knife, rolling pin, 8 cm round cookie cutter

INGREDIENTS

8 pitted, dried dates (regular-sized dates, not the larger Medjool dates)

5 tbsp soft cream cheese (not low-fat or fat-free) (see "Cream Cheese," page 16)

4 tbsp soft unsalted butter (see "Butter," page 16)

4 tbsp white sugar

1 egg white (see "Eggs," page 16)

½ tsp white vinegar

½ tsp vanilla extract

pinch of salt

250 ml (1 cup) plain flour (spoon in, level; see page 19)

16 white chocolate baking wafers

Tuck dried dates and white chocolate inside an envelope of pastry dough. These are best when they're lukewarm and the date is soft and sticky.

① Preheat the oven to 170°C/150°C fan/gas 3. Line a baking sheet with parchment paper. Also cut two other large pieces of parchment.

② Use kitchen scissors to cut the dates in half lengthwise—that means into two long halves, not two short ones. Ask a helper to explain if you don't know what this means. Set aside.

③ In a large bowl, use the back of a wooden spoon to cream together the cream cheese, butter, and sugar. Mix in the egg white, vinegar, vanilla, and salt until smooth.

④ Gradually stir the flour into the cream cheese mixture to form a soft dough. Use a dinner knife to scrape sticky ingredients off the spoon. When it gets too stiff to stir, use your hands to press any crumbly bits into the dough—keeping the dough in the bowl. The dough will be soft but not sticky.

⑤ Use the dinner knife to cut the dough into two equal-sized pieces. Place one piece between the two sheets of parchment you cut in step 1. Put your rolling pin on the top piece of parchment and roll out the dough to 5 mm thick (see "Two-Stacked-Pound-Coins Rule," page 19).

⑥ Use the cookie cutter to cut circles in the dough. The circles can be touching, but not overlapping.

⑦ Place a white chocolate wafer in the middle of each circle of dough, then put a date half on top of each wafer. Use a dinner knife to help you lift up the edges of the dough. Pull two opposite sides of the circle of dough over the date and tightly pinch the edges shut (this is easiest to do if you pull up the dough along the length of the date, not its width). You will end up with half-moon-shaped pockets. Set them onto the baking sheet about 5 cm apart. Squeeze together the dough scraps and set aside.

CONTINUED ON PAGE 159

SWEET DATE POCKETS

Sweet Date Pockets (cont'd)

(8) Make more Sweet Date Pockets with the second piece of dough and set them on the parchment. Squeeze together all your dough scraps, roll them out and make a few more of the cookies. Place them on the parchment, too. You should have 15 or 16 Sweet Date Pockets.

(9) Bake on the middle rack of the oven for 35 to 40 minutes, until they have just a few golden touches. Cool on the baking sheet until lukewarm before eating.

Makes 15 or 16 Sweet Date Pockets.

Cocoa Cranberry Crack-Ups

SUPPLIES

2 baking sheets, parchment paper, bowls, sieve, measuring cups, measuring spoons, baking spatula, wooden spoon, dinner knife

INGREDIENTS

185 ml (¾ cup) plain flour (spoon in, level; see page 19)

5 tbsp unsweetened cocoa powder (spoon in, level)

½ tsp baking powder

pinch of salt

4 tbsp unsalted butter

125 ml (½ cup) white sugar

½ tsp vanilla extract

1 egg

5 tbsp chocolate chips

4 tbsp dried cranberries or dried cherries

125 ml (½ cup) icing sugar (spoon in, level)

These icing-sugar-dusted cookies stay soft, almost cakey, in the middle.

1. Preheat the oven to 180°C/160°C fan/gas 4.

2. Line the baking sheets with parchment paper. (If you have only one baking sheet, after baking the first batch let the sheet cool before using it again.)

3. In a big bowl, sift the flour, cocoa powder, baking powder, and salt. Mix with a baking spatula and set aside.

4. In another large, microwave-safe bowl, melt the butter in the microwave at 50% power (about 1 minute). Use a wooden spoon to blend in the white sugar and vanilla. Mix in the egg.

5. Pour the cocoa mixture into the butter mixture. Mix until you have an evenly coloured cocoa dough. Use a dinner knife to scrape sticky ingredients off the wooden spoon. Stir in the chocolate chips and dried cranberries or cherries. Test the dough by pressing on it. If the dough sticks to your fingers, let it sit on the counter for 5 or 10 minutes to firm up. It will get less sticky.

6. Sift the icing sugar into a bowl. Set aside.

7. Press the dough into level tablespoons. Push the dough out of the spoon with your finger and roll it into a ball. Roll each ball in the icing sugar to cover completely. Hold the balls loosely in your cupped hand and shake off the bigger lumps of sugar. Place the balls on the parchment. Make 20 sugar-covered balls.

8. Next, roll each ball a *second* time in the icing sugar. Shake off the extra sugar. Place the balls about 5 cm apart on the baking sheets. Put ten on each sheet.

9. Bake, one sheet at a time for 10 minutes, until small cracks appear on the cookies. Cool completely before eating.

Makes 20 Cocoa Cranberry Crack-Ups.

COCOA CRANBERRY CRACK-UPS

DARK CHOCOLATE CRISPS

Dark Chocolate Crisps

SUPPLIES

bowls, measuring cups, measuring spoons, sieve, wooden spoon, dinner knife, cling film, 2 baking sheets, parchment paper, rolling pin, cookie cutters

INGREDIENTS

185 ml (¾ cup) plain flour (spoon in, level; see page 19)

4 tbsp + 1 tbsp whole wheat flour (spoon in, level)

½ tsp baking soda

⅛ tsp salt

4 tbsp unsweetened cocoa powder (spoon in, level)

125 ml (½ cup) soft unsalted butter (see "Butter," page 16)

125 ml (½ cup) firmly packed dark brown sugar

1 tbsp runny honey

1 tsp vanilla extract

assorted baking sprinkles, if you wish

Thin, crunchy cookies made for munching with a glass of cold milk.

1. In a bowl, using a wooden spoon, stir together the plain and whole wheat flours, baking soda, and salt. Sift in the cocoa powder and mix well. Set aside.

2. In another large bowl, use the back of the wooden spoon to cream together the butter, brown sugar, honey, and vanilla.

3. Stir two or three spoonfuls of the cocoa mixture at a time into the butter mixture, until all the cocoa mixture is added. Use a dinner knife to scrape sticky ingredients off the spoon. This mixture turns into a soft dough. Use your hands to press any crumbly bits in the bottom of the bowl into the dough. Cover the bowl with cling film and chill for 30 minutes.

4. After the dough has chilled, preheat the oven to 170°C/150°C fan/gas 3.

5. Line the baking sheets with parchment paper. (If you have only one baking sheet, cool if off after baking the first batch before using it again.) Also cut two other large pieces of parchment paper.

6. Use the dinner knife to cut the chilled dough into two pieces. Tuck one piece of dough between the two sheets of parchment paper you cut in the previous step. Put your rolling pin on the top piece of parchment and roll the dough to 5 mm thick (see "Two-Stacked-Pound-Coins Rule," page 19).

7. Cut shapes in the rolled dough with a cookie cutter. Lift off the cutouts with a dinner knife and place on the baking sheets 2.5 cm apart. Gently pat the baking sprinkles, if using, on top. Press the scraps of dough onto the second piece of dough. Roll, cut, and decorate the same way.

8. Bake, one sheet at a time, on the middle rack of the oven for 10 to 12 minutes, until the cookies are no longer shiny. Cool completely on the baking sheets.

Makes about 28 Dark Chocolate Crisps.

Finnigans

SUPPLIES

bowls, baking spatula, measuring cups, measuring spoons, wooden spoon, dinner knife, cling film, 2 baking sheets, parchment paper, rolling pin, cookie cutter

INGREDIENTS

185 ml (¾ cup) plain flour (spoon in, level; see page 19)

125 ml (½ cup) whole wheat flour (spoon in, level)

2 tbsp wheat germ

½ tsp baking soda

¼ tsp ground cinnamon

¼ tsp salt

pinch of nutmeg

125 ml (½ cup) soft unsalted butter (see "Butter," page 16)

125 ml (½ cup) firmly packed light brown sugar

1 tbsp runny honey

½ tsp vanilla extract

¼ tsp lemon extract

Glossy Cookie Glaze and/or silver dragées, if you like

Crisp, buttery cookies that taste like honey, cinnamon, and lemons. A pet goldfish, Finnigan, inspired the fish-shaped cutter—and the name for the cookies! But you can cut your cookies into any shape you wish. Decorate with silver balls called dragées and/or Glossy Cookie Glaze (page 156).

1. In a bowl and using a baking spatula, mix the all-purpose and whole wheat flours, wheat germ, baking soda, cinnamon, salt, and nutmeg. Set aside.

2. In another large bowl, use the back of a wooden spoon to cream together the butter, brown sugar, honey, vanilla, and lemon extract. Switch to the baking spatula and gradually mix the flour mixture into the butter mixture. Use a dinner knife to scrape sticky ingredients off the spatula. When the dough becomes too stiff to stir, use your hands to squeeze in the dry crumbly bits. Leaving the dough in the bowl, press the dough into a ball. Cover the bowl with cling film and chill for 30 minutes.

3. After the dough has chilled, preheat the oven to 180°C/160°C fan/gas 4.

4. Line the baking sheets with parchment paper. (If you have only one baking sheet, after baking the first batch let the sheet cool before using it again.) Also cut two other large pieces of parchment paper.

5. Use a dinner knife to cut the chilled dough into two pieces. Tuck a piece between the two sheets of parchment paper you cut in the previous step. Put your rolling pin on the top piece of parchment and roll out the dough to 5 mm thick (see "Two-Stacked-Pound-Coins Rule," page 19).

6. Cut shapes in the rolled dough with the cookie cutter. Lift off the cutouts with the dinner knife and set them on the baking sheets 2.5 cm apart. Press the scraps into the second piece of dough. Roll and cut the same way.

CONTINUED ON NEXT PAGE

7. Fill up both baking sheets. If you want to decorate with silver dragées but not with glaze, press the dragées onto the dough now. (If you are going to use the glaze and dragées, you should bake and cool the cookies, glaze them, then stick the dragées onto the wet glaze.)

8. Bake, one sheet at a time, for 8 to 10 minutes, until the cookies are golden at the edges. Cool completely on the baking sheets before glazing or eating.

Makes about 24 Finnigans.

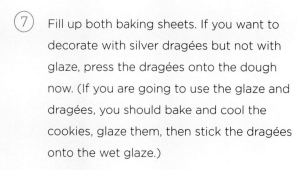

COOKIE TORTOISES

Cookie Tortoises

[GF]

SUPPLIES

baking sheet, parchment paper, bowl, wooden spoon, measuring spoons

INGREDIENTS

3 tbsp smooth peanut butter

3 tbsp packed brown sugar

1 egg yolk (see "Eggs," page 16)

24 walnut halves

24 chocolate baking wafers

Who can resist these bite-sized treats made by layering peanut butter cookie dough and chocolate onto walnuts?

1. Preheat the oven to 170°C/150°C fan/gas 3.

2. Line a baking sheet with parchment paper.

3. In a bowl, use a wooden spoon to mix the peanut butter (if you have the kind where the oil and peanuts are separate, mix them before you measure out what you need), brown sugar, and egg yolk into a smooth, glossy, soft peanut butter dough.

4. Pinch off pieces of the cookie dough to fill a ½ teaspoon level, then roll the dough into balls. If the dough is too soft to roll, mix in another tablespoon or two of brown sugar.

5. Place each cookie dough ball onto a walnut half, then gently flatten it onto the nut with the palm of your hand until the dough is 6 mm thick and covers the top of the walnut half. Do this for all 24 walnut halves. Place the dough-topped walnut halves 2.5 cm apart on the parchment-lined baking sheet.

6. Bake on the middle rack of the oven for 10 minutes. Remove from the oven (but keep the oven on) and cool until the baking sheet is safe to work with.

7. Place one chocolate wafer on top of each dough-topped walnut. Put the baking sheet back into the oven for 1 minute to slightly melt the chocolate onto the peanut butter cookie layer.

8. Cool the cookies to room temperature, then chill in the fridge for 5 minutes to firm up the chocolate before eating.

Makes 24 Cookie Tortoises.

Nuterettis

[GF]

SUPPLIES

baking sheet, parchment paper, bowls, baking spatula, measuring cups, measuring spoons, dinner knife, cooling rack

INGREDIENTS

185 ml (¾ cup) + 2 tbsp ground hazelnuts

125 ml (½ cup) brown rice flour (or white rice flour, regular, not glutinous) (spoon in, level; see page 19)

5 tbsp firmly packed light brown sugar

⅛ tsp baking soda

pinch of salt

2 egg yolks (see "Eggs," page 16)

2 tbsp maple syrup

½ tsp lemon juice

¼ tsp almond extract

Similar to Italian cookies called amaretti, these nutty goodies with soft middles get their toasty taste from hazelnuts. You could also use ground pecans, walnuts, or almonds.

① Preheat the oven to 150°C/130°C fan/gas 2.

② Line a baking sheet with parchment paper.

③ In a bowl and using a baking spatula, mix the ground hazelnuts, rice flour, brown sugar, baking soda, and salt. Set aside.

④ In another large bowl, use the baking spatula to blend together the egg yolks, maple syrup, lemon juice, and almond extract. Use a dinner knife to scrape sticky ingredients off the spatula. Gradually stir in the hazelnut mixture. If it gets too stiff to stir, use your hands to squeeze the mixture into a dough. Make sure the ingredients are mixed well.

⑤ To make each cookie, pinch off enough dough to press into a level tablespoon. Push the dough out of the spoon with your finger and roll each spoonful into a ball (wet your hands with cold water before doing this, because the dough is a little sticky). Make 16 balls. Set them about 5 cm apart on the parchment-lined baking sheet.

⑥ Bake on the middle rack of the oven for 22 minutes, or until the cookies puff up, get little cracks around the edges, and turn lightly golden. Cool slightly, then place the cookies on a cooling rack until they are just barely warm before eating.

Makes 16 Nuterettis.

NUTERETTIS

Sugar Delights

[GF]

SUPPLIES

bowls, sieve, measuring cups, measuring spoons, wooden spoon, dinner knife, cling film, 2 baking sheets, parchment paper, rolling pin, cookie cutters

INGREDIENTS

185 ml (¾ cup) white rice flour (glutinous; see "Rice Flour," page 18) (spoon in, level; see page 19)

3 tbsp tapioca starch

2 tbsp sorghum flour

¼ tsp baking powder

⅛ tsp baking soda

pinch of salt

5 tbsp white sugar

4 tbsp soft unsalted butter (see "Butter," page 16)

1 egg white (see "Eggs," page 16)

1 tsp milk

½ tsp vanilla extract

2 tbsp cornflour

Glossy Cookie Glaze, if you like

Wonderfully light and crunchy, these treats are the gluten-free version of traditional sugar cookies. Decorate with Glossy Cookie Glaze (page 156), if you like.

① In a bowl, sift together the rice flour, tapioca starch, sorghum flour, baking powder, baking soda, and salt. Mix with a wooden spoon. Set aside.

② In a large bowl, use the back of the wooden spoon to cream together the sugar and butter until smooth. Mix in the egg white, milk, and vanilla. Gradually stir the flour mixture into the butter mixture to form a soft dough. Use a dinner knife to scrape sticky ingredients off the spoon. Set aside.

③ Into another bowl, sift the cornflour. This is the special ingredient that makes the dough the perfect texture for rolling. Gradually stir spoonfuls of the cornflour into the dough. When the dough becomes too stiff to stir, use your hands to squeeze in the rest of the cornflour. You might not need it all; stop when the dough is soft but doesn't stick to your hands. Make sure the ingredients are mixed together evenly. (If the dough is too dry, add another ¼ tsp milk. If it is a little too sticky, add another 1 tsp of sifted cornflour.)

④ Press the dough into a ball and leave it in the bowl. Cover with cling film and chill for 30 minutes.

⑤ After the dough has chilled, preheat the oven to 190°C/170°C fan/gas 5.

⑥ Line the baking sheets with parchment paper. (If you have only one baking sheet, let the sheet cool before using it again.) Also cut two other large pieces of parchment.

⑦ Use the dinner knife to cut the chilled dough into two pieces. Cover one piece and put it back in the refrigerator, and tuck the other piece between the two sheets of parchment you cut in the previous step. Put your rolling pin on the top piece of parchment and roll out the dough to 5 mm thick (see "Two-Stacked-Pound-Coins Rule," page 19).

CONTINUED ON PAGE 172

CLOCKWISE FROM TOP LEFT:
BROWN SUGAR CRINKLES (PAGE 174),
SUGAR DELIGHTS WITH GLOSSY COOKIE GLAZE (PAGE 156),
CHOCOLATE RONDELLES (PAGE 173)

Sugar Delights (cont'd)

(8) Cut shapes in the rolled dough with the cookie cutter. Lift the cutouts with the dinner knife and set them on the parchment-lined baking sheets 2.5 cm apart. Press the scraps into the second piece of dough. Roll and cut the second piece in the same way as the first.

(9) Bake, one sheet at a time, on the middle rack of the oven for 8 to 10 minutes, until the cookies are golden at the edges. Cool completely on the baking sheets before glazing or eating.

Makes about 24 Sugar Delights.

Chocolate Rondelles

[GF]

SUPPLIES

2 baking sheets, parchment paper, bowls, sieve, measuring cups, measuring spoons, whisk, wooden spoon, dinner knife

INGREDIENTS

125 ml (½ cup) chickpea flour (also known as garbanzo bean flour) (spoon in, level; see page 19)

125 ml (½ cup) cornflour (spoon in, level)

5 tbsp white rice flour (regular, not glutinous) (spoon in, level)

4 tbsp unsweetened cocoa powder (spoon in, level)

½ tsp unflavoured gelatin powder

¼ tsp baking soda

pinch of salt

125 ml (½ cup) firmly packed brown sugar

5 tbsp soft unsalted butter (see "Butter," page 16)

4 tbsp white sugar

1 egg

2 tbsp runny honey

1 tsp vanilla extract

5 tbsp chocolate chips

_____

PICTURED ON PAGE 171

Why "rondelles"? *Rondelles de hockey* is the French-Canadian phrase for "hockey pucks," which are the same diameter as these soft and moist treats that everyone will love!

1. Preheat the oven to 180°C/160°C fan/gas 4.

2. Line the baking sheets with parchment paper. (If you have only one baking sheet, let the sheet cool before refilling it with the second batch of cookie dough.)

3. In a bowl, sift in the chickpea flour, cornflour, rice flour, cocoa powder, gelatin powder, baking soda, and salt. Mix well with a whisk. Set aside.

4. In a big bowl, use the back of a wooden spoon to cream together the brown sugar, butter, and white sugar. Switch to the whisk and mix in the egg, honey, and vanilla until smooth.

5. Use the spoon to gradually stir the flour mixture into the butter mixture until a soft dough forms. Use a dinner knife to scrape sticky ingredients off the spoon

6. Mix in the chocolate chips.

7. Use a tablespoon to scoop mounds of the dough onto the parchment-lined sheets, pushing the dough off the spoon with your finger. Make 16 mounds about 8 cm apart. Don't flatten the dough.

8. Bake, one sheet at a time, on the middle rack of the oven for 10 to 12 minutes, or until the edges of the cookies are firm and the tops of the cookies don't look shiny anymore. Cool on the baking sheets.

Makes 16 Chocolate Rondelles.

Brown Sugar Crinkles

[GF]

SUPPLIES

baking sheet, parchment paper, bowls, wooden spoon, measuring cups, measuring spoons, sieve, baking spatula, dinner knife, small dish

INGREDIENTS

4 tbsp soft unsalted butter (see "Butter," page 16)

5 tbsp firmly packed light brown sugar

1 tbsp white sugar

1 egg yolk (see "Eggs," page 16)

½ tsp vanilla extract

160 ml (⅔ cup) brown rice flour (spoon in, level; see page 19)

2 tbsp potato starch

½ tsp unflavoured gelatin powder

¼ tsp baking soda

pinch of salt

2 tbsp coloured coarse sugar

PICTURED ON PAGE 171

You decorate these cookies before they go into the oven! Look for coloured sugars in the baking aisle of the grocery store.

1. Preheat the oven to 170°C/150°C fan/gas 3.

2. Line a baking sheet with parchment paper. Set aside.

3. In a small bowl, use the back of a wooden spoon to cream together the butter, brown sugar, and white sugar. Mix in the egg yolk and vanilla until smooth. Set aside.

4. In another bowl, sift in the rice flour, potato starch, gelatin powder, baking soda, and salt (don't add the coarse sugar yet). Mix well with a baking spatula.

5. Use the spatula to gradually stir the flour mixture into the butter mixture to form a dough. Use a dinner knife to scrape sticky ingredients off the spatula. When it gets too stiff to stir, use your hands to squeeze in the dry bits—keeping the dough in the bowl. It will be a soft, but not sticky, dough. Set aside.

6. Put the coarse sugar in a small dish.

7. To shape the cookies, fill a level tablespoon with dough. Pull it out of the spoon with your finger and roll it into a ball. Dip one half of the dough ball into the coarse sugar. Then place the ball—sugar-side up—on the parchment paper. Fill, roll, and dip the rest of the dough in the same way. Be sure to dip each ball of dough in the sugar right after you roll it so the dough is still moist and the sugar will stick to it easily. Make 13 sugar-coated balls. Place them on the parchment paper evenly spaced apart.

8. Bake 15 to 16 minutes, until the cookies spread, turn lightly golden and little cracks appear on them. Cool on the baking sheet until lukewarm before eating.

Makes 13 Brown Sugar Crinkles.

Peanut Butter Beezies

[GF]

SUPPLIES

baking sheet, parchment paper, bowl, wooden spoon, measuring cups, baking spatula, measuring spoons, dinner knife, ordinary teaspoon

INGREDIENTS

125 ml (½ cup) crunchy, all-natural
  peanut butter
125 ml (½ cup) firmly packed brown
  sugar
1 egg
½ tsp vanilla extract
heaped 1 tbsp cherry, raspberry, or
  strawberry jam, if
  you like

PICTURED ON PAGE 150

You need only four ingredients to make these yummy cookies, five if you want jam.

1. Preheat the oven to 170°C/150°C fan/gas 3.

2. Line a baking sheet with parchment paper.

3. Before measuring the peanut butter, stir it if it's the kind where the oil sits on top of the peanut butter.

4. In a bowl, use the back of a wooden spoon to cream together the peanut butter and brown sugar. Then stir in the egg and vanilla until you have a soft, well-mixed dough. Use a dinner knife to scrape sticky ingredients off the spoon. Depending on how stiff your peanut butter is, you'll have either a stiff, non-sticky dough or a soft, spreadable dough.

5. If your dough is stiff, fill a tablespoon level with the dough. Push it out with your finger and roll it into a ball. Put the balls on the parchment-lined baking sheet, then press them down with your palm to flatten into 1 cm thick rounds. If the dough is soft, use an ordinary teaspoon to scoop heaped spoonfuls and drop into 14 mounds on the parchment. Keep the dough about 5 cm apart.

6. If you want to make these cookies without adding any jam, bake them for 17 to 18 minutes until the edges are lightly browned. Cool on the baking sheet before eating.

7. If you would like to add jam to the tops of the cookies, first bake the cookies on the middle rack of the oven for 12 minutes, then remove them from the oven (but keep the oven on). Cool the baking sheet slightly so it's safe to work with.

8. Gently press the bottom of a ¼ teaspoon into the top of each cookie to make a little dimple. Use the same ¼ teaspoon to fill each dimple with jam. Put the cookies back in the oven for 8 to 10 minutes, until they are lightly browned at the edges. Cool on the baking sheet until the jam firms up.

Makes 14 Peanut Butter Beezies.

your sweet treats

● ● ● ● ● ●

Make delightfully unique goodies
for your sweet tooth!

ALMOND-OAT BAKED APPLES

Almond-Oat Baked Apples

SUPPLIES

bowl, wooden spoon, measuring cups, measuring spoons, knife (for helper), apple corer (for helper), 20 cm square glass or ceramic baking dish

INGREDIENTS

4 tbsp soft unsalted butter (see "Butter," page 16)

4 tbsp firmly packed light or dark brown sugar

5 tbsp ground almonds

5 tbsp rolled oats, traditional or quick-cooking (but not instant)

¼ tsp ground cinnamon

pinch of nutmeg

2 baking apples

125 ml water

vanilla ice cream or whipped cream for serving, if you like

Instead of whole baked apples, these are halves—just the right kid-sized serving.

1. Preheat the oven to 190°C/170°C fan/gas 5.

2. In a bowl, use the back of a wooden spoon to cream together the butter and brown sugar. Mix in the ground almonds, rolled oats, cinnamon, and nutmeg. Set aside.

3. Keep the skins on the apples. Get help cutting the apples in half crosswise (horizontally across the core) and coring each half.

4. Place the four apple halves—cut sides facing up—in the baking dish.

5. Push the oat mixture into the empty cores, then press into mounds on top of the apple halves.

6. Carefully pour the water into the baking dish, but don't get water on the oat mixture.

7. Bake on the middle rack of the oven for 40 minutes, or until the oat mixture is lightly golden. Cool the apples to lukewarm, then place in serving dishes. Eat with a dollop of vanilla ice cream or whipped cream, if you like.

Makes 4 Almond-Oat Baked Apples.

Peaches in Pastry Nests

SUPPLIES

baking sheet, parchment paper, sieve, can opener, bowls, wooden spoon, measuring cups, measuring spoons, dinner knife, rolling pin, pastry brush

INGREDIENTS

4 canned peach halves

4 tbsp soft cream cheese (see "Cream cheese," page 16)

2 tbsp soft unsalted butter (see "Butter," page 16)

2 tbsp white sugar

¼ tsp white vinegar

pinch of salt

125 ml (½ cup) plain flour (spoon in, level; see page 19)

2 tbsp apricot or peach jam

For a treat that tastes like old-fashioned fruit pie, wrap peach halves in this buttery pastry.

1. Preheat the oven to 180°C/160°C fan/gas 4.

2. Line a baking sheet with parchment paper. Also cut another two large pieces of parchment for use in a later step.

3. Put the sieve over a big bowl. Open the can of peaches and pour the fruit into the sieve to drain. Set the peaches aside. Throw away the liquid.

4. In another large bowl, use the back of a wooden spoon to cream together the cream cheese, butter, and sugar. Mix in the vinegar and salt.

5. Gradually stir the flour into the cream cheese mixture to form a dough. Use your hands to press it into a disk. If it sticks to your hands, sprinkle on another small spoonful of flour and squeeze it into the dough.

6. Use a dinner knife to cut the dough into four equal pieces. Roll each piece into a ball. Place each dough ball, one at a time, between the two pieces of parchment paper you cut in step 2. Place the rolling pin over the top sheet of parchment and roll the dough into a circle about 12 cm across and 5 mm thick (see "Two-Stacked-Pound-Coins Rule," page 19). Peel off each dough circle and set on the parchment-lined sheet. Roll out all four balls of dough.

7. Place a peach half—rounded side facing up—in the centre of each circle of dough. Scrunch the dough up and around the sides of the peach halves, leaving the tops peeking out.

8. Bake for 30 to 35 minutes, or until the pastry is lightly golden. Cool until just warm.

9. Place the jam in a microwave-safe bowl and heat in the microwave at 50% power until runny (about 30 seconds). Dip a pastry brush into the jam and brush it onto the four peach halves to make them shiny.

Makes 4 Peaches in Pastry Nests.

Apple Crisp

SUPPLIES

bowls, wooden spoon, measuring cups, measuring spoons, dinner knife, knife (for helper), 20 cm square microwave-safe glass or ceramic baking dish, baking spatula

INGREDIENTS

TOPPING

125 ml (½ cup) soft unsalted butter (see "Butter," page 16)

125 ml (½ cup) firmly packed brown sugar

1 tbsp white sugar

pinch of salt

250 ml (1 cup) rolled oats, traditional or quick-cooking (but not instant)

160 ml (⅔ cup) plain flour (spoon in, level; see page 19)

APPLE LAYER

3 baking apples

1 tbsp unsalted butter

2 tbsp white sugar

¼ tsp ground cinnamon

You'll need a helper to peel and cut the apples, but you get to do the rest of the recipe! Your kitchen will smell so amazing!

1. Preheat the oven to 190°C/170°C fan/gas 5.

2. In a large bowl, use the back of a wooden spoon to cream together the butter, brown sugar, 1 tbsp white sugar, and salt.

3. Add the rolled oats and flour to the butter mixture and stir until the mixture is crumbly and no dry flour can be seen. Use a dinner knife to scrape sticky ingredients from the wooden spoon. Don't be afraid to use your hands to mix the ingredients together more quickly. Set aside.

4. Ask a helper to peel and cut the apples into 2.5 cm chunks.

5. Meanwhile, put the 1 tbsp butter into the baking dish and heat in the microwave at 50% power until melted (about 30 seconds). Tilt the baking dish to roll the melted butter around the bottom, or use a baking spatula to spread the melted butter.

6. Spread the apple chunks in the baking dish.

7. In a small bowl, mix the 2 tbsp white sugar and the cinnamon. Sprinkle over the apple.

8. Sprinkle the rolled oats mixture evenly on the apples. Don't worry if there are some lumps.

9. Bake on the middle rack of the oven for 30 to 35 minutes, or until the rolled oats are golden.

Serves 6.

APPLE CRISP

FRUIT FRITTERS

Fruit Fritters

[GF]

SUPPLIES

rimmed baking sheet, parchment paper, bowl, measuring cup, measuring spoons, pastry brush or cling film, whisk, sieve, dinner knife (if using a banana) or knife (for helper) if using an apple, cooking spatula (for helper)

INGREDIENTS

4 tbsp unsalted butter

2 tsp white sugar

pinch of salt

125 ml (½ cup) cornflour (spoon in, level; see page 19)

¼ tsp baking soda

2 egg whites (see "Eggs," page 16)

1 banana or 1 green apple

First, you have to make a hard decision: do you want to make banana fritters or green apple fritters? They're both good. The fruit turns soft and sweet in the oven, coated in a golden, crispy batter.

1. Preheat the oven to 190°C/170°C fan/gas 5.

2. Line a baking sheet with parchment paper.

3. In a large microwave-safe bowl, heat the butter at 50% power in the microwave until melted (about 1 minute). Drizzle 2 tbsp of the butter on the parchment paper. Use a pastry brush or scrunched-up piece of cling film to rub the butter all over the parchment, leaving about a 5 cm unbuttered border around the edges. Set aside.

4. You will have 2 tbsp melted butter left in the bowl. To make the batter, use a whisk to stir the white sugar and salt into the bowl of butter. Set the whisk aside. Carefully sift the cornflour and baking soda into the same bowl. Then add the egg whites. Use the whisk to stir into a smooth batter.

5. If you are using a banana, peel it and use a dinner knife to cut it into 1 cm rounds. If you are using an apple, get help peeling it and slicing into 1 cm thick wedges.

6. Put three pieces of fruit into the batter at a time. Using your fingers, carefully roll them around to coat them in batter. Pick up one piece at a time, letting the extra batter drip back into the bowl. Put the fruit on the buttered parchment. Coat all the fruit in the same way. Don't let the pieces touch as you fill up the baking sheet. You probably won't use up all the batter.

7. Bake the coated pieces of fruit for 6 minutes. Get help turning them over with a cooking spatula, then bake another 5 to 6 minutes, until the batter is golden. Cool slightly but eat while warm.

Makes 10 to 12 Fruit Fritters.

Warm Caramel Banana Sundaes

[GF]

SUPPLIES

baking spatula, measuring cups, 20 cm square—or similar size—glass or ceramic baking dish with lid (or foil), dinner knife, measuring spoons

INGREDIENTS

5 tbsp single cream (10% milk fat)

4 tbsp packed brown sugar

pinch of salt

2 firm bananas

2 tbsp chocolate chips and/or butterscotch chips

2 tbsp sliced or slivered almonds, if you wish

ice cream for serving

Serve this warm topping over your favourite ice cream. The bananas and chips soften as the cream and brown sugar cook into a caramel sauce.

1. Preheat the oven to 190°C/170°C fan/gas 5.

2. Using a baking spatula, mix the cream, brown sugar, and salt in the baking dish.

3. Peel the bananas. Use a dinner knife to cut each banana in thirds. Then cut each third in half lengthwise. You will have twelve pieces. Use your fingers to roll the pieces in the cream mixture and spread them out in the baking dish. Don't overlap them.

4. Sprinkle the chocolate and/or butterscotch chips and almonds, if using, on top of the bananas and cream mixture. Cover the dish with the lid or foil.

5. Bake on the middle rack of the oven for 15 to 18 minutes. Get help checking that the caramel sauce has thickened. Get help removing the dish from the oven. Uncover and cool until just warm.

6. Scoop ice cream into four bowls or sundae cups. Spoon the warm topping over the ice cream. Eat right away while the bananas are soft.

Makes 4 Warm Caramel Banana Sundaes.

WARM CARAMEL BANANA SUNDAES

Fresh Berry Shortcakes

SUPPLIES

baking sheet, parchment paper, bowls, wooden spoon, measuring cups, measuring spoons, baking spatula, dinner knife, cooking spatula (for helper), sieve

INGREDIENTS

5 tbsp ricotta cheese (preferably extra smooth)

4 tbsp soft unsalted butter (see "Butter," page 16)

160 ml (⅔ cup) white sugar

1 egg

½ tsp vanilla extract

250 ml (1 cup) plain flour (spoon in, level; see page 19)

¼ tsp baking soda

pinch of salt

250 ml whipped cream or 4 scoops vanilla ice cream

250 ml (1 cup) raspberries or sliced strawberries

½ tsp icing sugar, if you like

These look a bit like pancakes, but they're soft, sweet little sponge cakes that go well with berries. They're best fresh, so eat them right after you make them.

1. Preheat the oven to 150°C/130°C fan/gas 2.

2. Line a baking sheet with parchment paper.

3. In a large bowl, use a wooden spoon to stir together the ricotta and butter. Use the back of the spoon to cream in the sugar. Then mix in the egg and vanilla extract. Set aside.

4. In another bowl, use a baking spatula to mix the flour, baking soda, and salt. Gradually, use the spatula to stir this dry mixture into the ricotta mixture. Mix into a stiff batter. Use a dinner knife to scrape sticky ingredients off the spatula.

5. Use the wooden spoon to scoop the batter into eight equal-sized mounds on the parchment, using your finger to scrape the batter off the spoon. Make sure to keep the mounds about 8 cm apart because the shortcakes spread during baking.

6. Bake on the middle rack of the oven for 13 to 15 minutes, until the shortcakes stop spreading and they turn golden like the colour of pancakes. Get help turning the shortcakes over with a cooking spatula and bake for another 12 to 13 minutes, until lightly golden. Cool on the baking sheet.

7. Put four shortcakes into four dessert dishes. Top each cake with whipped cream or ice cream and berries. Place the other four shortcakes on top. Using a sieve, dust each one with icing sugar, if you like.

Makes 4 Fresh Berry Shortcakes.

FRESH BERRY SHORTCAKES

Whoopie Pies

SUPPLIES

baking sheet, parchment paper, bowls, wooden spoon, measuring cups, measuring spoons, sieve, baking spatula, dinner knife, soup spoon, ordinary teaspoon, dinner knife or palette knife

INGREDIENTS

5 tbsp ricotta cheese (preferably extra smooth)

4 tbsp soft unsalted butter (see "Butter," page 16)

160 ml (⅔ cup) white sugar

1 egg

½ tsp vanilla extract

185 ml (¾ cup) plain flour (spoon in, level; see page 19)

4 tbsp unsweetened cocoa powder (spoon in, level)

¼ tsp baking soda

pinch of salt

Whoopie Pie Filling (see page 192) or your choice of frosting or ice cream

These aren't pies at all. They're disks of chocolate cake made into sweet, frosting-filled sandwiches. The ricotta doesn't taste like cheese—it makes the cakes fluffy!

1. Preheat the oven to 170°C/150°C fan/gas 3.

2. Line a baking sheet with parchment paper.

3. In a large bowl, use the back of a wooden spoon to cream together the ricotta cheese and butter. Mix in the sugar, egg, and vanilla. Use a dinner knife to clean off the spoon. Set aside.

4. In another big bowl, sift the flour, cocoa powder, baking soda, and salt. Mix well with a baking spatula. Gradually stir this mixture into the ricotta mixture. Use a dinner knife to scrape sticky ingredients off the spatula so everything is well blended into a batter.

5. Use a soup spoon to scoop the batter and push it off with your finger onto the parchment. Make eight equal-sized dollops, keeping the dollops at least 5 cm apart because they spread a lot as they bake. The tops of the dollops will be bumpy. If you want your whoopie pies to be smooth on top, smooth out the bumps before baking by dipping an ordinary teaspoon in cold water and lightly running the back of the spoon over the big bumps—but don't squash the batter.

6. Bake on the middle rack of the oven for about 14 minutes, or until the whoopie pies spring back when lightly pressed in the middle.

7. After the cakes have cooled completely on the baking sheet, use a dinner knife or palette knife to spread the flat sides of four cakes with Whoopie Pie Filling, 185 ml of other frosting, or even softened ice cream. Place the remaining four cakes on top of the filling and serve. (You could also eat the cakes plain.)

Makes 4 Whoopie Pies.

WHOOPIE PIES AND
WHOOPIE PIE FILLING (PAGE 192)

WHOOPIE PIE FILLING [GF]

SUPPLIES

sieve, measuring cups, bowls, measuring spoons, drinking cup or small dish, wooden spoon, ordinary teaspoon

INGREDIENTS

375 ml (1½ cups) icing sugar (spoon in, level; see page 19)

2 tbsp cream or milk

2 tbsp soft unsalted butter (see "Butter," page 16)

pinch of salt

PICTURED ON PAGE 190

1. Sift the icing sugar into a bowl. Set aside.

2. Measure the cream or milk into a drinking cup or small dish. Set aside.

3. In a large bowl, use the back of a wooden spoon to cream the butter and salt until the mixture is very soft.

4. To finish making the filling, you will switch back and forth between mixing in a little icing sugar and a little cream (or milk) into the butter mixture. Begin by using an ordinary teaspoon to add a few heaped spoonfuls of the icing sugar to the butter mixture. Cream them in with the back of the wooden spoon. Then add a small splash of cream (or milk) and mix in with the wooden spoon. Switch between mixing in spoonfuls of icing sugar and splashes of cream (or milk) until both are used up. Mix into a smooth frosting that holds its shape and isn't runny. If the filling is too soft, sift in a couple more tablespoons of icing sugar and mix in. If it is too stiff to spread, mix in about ⅛ tsp milk.

Makes enough frosting to fill 4 Whoopie Pies.

Sponge Toffee Lollipops

[GF]

SUPPLIES

2 rimmed baking sheets, parchment paper, bowls, sieve, measuring spoons, measuring cup, baking spatula, dinner knife, ordinary teaspoon, 7 wooden sticks or skewers (at least 15 cm long)

INGREDIENTS

3 tbsp icing sugar

⅛ tsp baking soda

4 tbsp instant skim milk powder
  (spoon in, level; see page 19)

3 tbsp firmly packed light brown sugar

1 tbsp whipping cream (35%)

2 tbsp runny honey

¼ tsp vanilla extract

pinch of salt

PICTURED ON PAGE 194

Are you ready for kitchen magic? This is the longest recipe in this book, but it doesn't take long to make! Be amazed as the batter turns into crunchy sponge toffee!

1. Preheat the oven to 120°C/100°C fan/gas ½.

2. Line the baking sheets with parchment paper. (In this recipe, it's important to have two baking sheets, since the batter might stiffen up too much in the bowl while you're waiting for the first baking sheet to cool off. If you have only one baking sheet, ask a friend or neighbour if you can borrow another—then thank them with a lollipop!)

3. In a big bowl, sift in the icing sugar and baking soda. Mix in the skim milk powder (don't sift this ingredient because it won't fit through the little holes of the sieve). Set aside.

4. In a big microwave-safe bowl and using a baking spatula, mix the light brown sugar, whipping cream, honey, vanilla, and salt. Heat in the microwave at 50% power for 30 seconds. Carefully remove from the microwave, stir, and heat again for 30 seconds at 50% power until the brown sugar is melted and the mixture is smooth (you may need to heat and stir once more to make sure the brown sugar is completely melted).

5. Gradually stir the icing sugar mixture into the melted brown sugar mixture. Mix well. It will turn into a sticky batter. Use a dinner knife to scrape sticky ingredients from the spatula so everything is well blended. The bits of milk powder don't have to melt completely.

6. Let the bowl of batter sit for 5 minutes before continuing with the recipe. Don't stir it or do anything else with it for 5 minutes—just be patient and wait. It's very important you do this step because—even though you can't see anything happening— something *is* happening to the ingredients that will help them turn into sponge candy later in the oven.

CONTINUED ON PAGE 195

SPONGE TOFFEE LOLLIPOPS

Sponge Toffee Lollipops (cont'd)

(7) Before you touch the batter, read this step first so you know how to do step 8 properly. The batter spreads like crazy when it bakes so it's very important to keep the blobs of batter well away from each other and the edges of the baking sheets. Use up all the batter to make seven lollipops. Each lollipop is made from about two spoonfuls of batter. Let the batter spread out slowly on its own, until it stops on its own. Don't try to spread it with your spoon.

(8) Okay. Now use an ordinary teaspoon to scoop the batter. Use your finger to push the blob of batter off the spoon onto the parchment. Drop another spoonful of batter right on top of the first one. They will spread into one circle. Let this pool of batter stop spreading before you start making another one, so you can leave enough space between blobs.

(9) Drop the next blobs at least 12 cm away from any batter already on the parchment and 5 cm from the edges of the baking sheet. Make three or four pools of batter on each sheet, for a total of seven. Try to use the same amount of batter for each pool.

(10) To add a handle to each lollipop, lay a wooden stick across the middle of each pool of batter. Make sure the wooden stick goes across the entire circle of batter and does not just stick part way into it. The more of the stick that's stuck into the batter, the better the lollipop will hold onto it after baking. Also, check that the handles of the sticks aren't too close to the other pools of batter.

(11) Use the handle of the teaspoon or another stick (or skewer) to press down on the lollipop sticks so they sink into the pools of batter. Don't be afraid to press down until the lollipop sticks almost touch the parchment paper. But they don't need to be covered by the batter.

(12) Bake, one sheet at a time, for 29 to 32 minutes, or until the sponge toffee is deeply golden. Watch them carefully in the last few minutes so they don't overbrown. The lollipops will puff up in the oven at first, then flatten out again as they turn crispy. Cool completely on the sheets to firm up before lifting off to eat. Do not touch them before they have cooled. Enjoy and share with others shortly after you make the lollipops because they soften up after an hour or two and aren't nearly as much fun to eat as when they're fresh and crunchy!

Makes 7 Sponge Toffee Lollipops.

BUTTERY GRANOLA BARS

Buttery Granola Bars

SUPPLIES

food processor (for helper), measuring cups, bowls, measuring spoons, 20 cm square glass, ceramic, or metal baking tin, foil, pastry brush or cling film, wooden spoon, dinner knife

INGREDIENTS

250 ml (1 cup) rolled oats, traditional or quick-cooking (but not instant)

5 tbsp plain flour (spoon in, level; see page 19)

4 tbsp unsalted sunflower seeds

½ tsp baking soda

¼ tsp salt

soft butter for foil

125 ml (½ cup) soft unsalted butter (see "Butter," page 16)

5 tbsp white sugar

5 tbsp firmly packed light brown sugar

1 egg yolk (see "Eggs," page 16)

½ tsp vanilla extract

A bit like granola bars and a bit like oatmeal cookies, too. Scrumptious!

1. Preheat the oven to 180°C/160°C fan/gas 4.

2. Get help to blitz the rolled oats in a food processor to the size of coarse salt and pour them into a big bowl. Now you can take over the work!

3. Use a wooden spoon to mix the flour, sunflower seeds, baking soda, and salt into the bowl of blitzed oats. Set aside.

4. Line the bottom and sides of the baking tin with a large sheet of foil. Use a pastry brush or a scrunched-up piece of cling film to butter the foil. Set aside.

5. In another big bowl, use the back of the wooden spoon to cream together the butter and the white and light brown sugars until blended. Then mix in the egg yolk and vanilla. Use a dinner knife to scrape sticky ingredients off the wooden spoon.

6. Stir the oat mixture into the butter mixture. Mix well.

7. Scoop the mixture into the buttered, foil-lined tin. Use the back of the wooden spoon to press the mixture evenly in the tin.

8. Bake on the middle rack of the oven for 25 minutes. The mixture will puff up during baking, then flatten out again. Cool in the tin until just slightly warm. Get help lifting out the foil together with the granola mixture. Peel off the foil and get help slicing the granola into bars or squares.

Makes about 20 Buttery Granola Bars.

Hazelnut Fudge Pebbles

[GF]

SUPPLIES

bowls, sieve, measuring cups, measuring spoons, baking spatula, dinner knife, plate

INGREDIENTS

250 ml (1 cup) icing sugar (spoon in, level; see page 19)

2 tbsp unsweetened cocoa powder

4 tbsp instant skim milk powder

1 tbsp unsalted butter

1 tbsp water

¼ tsp vanilla extract

22 hazelnuts, shells off

2 tbsp unsweetened cocoa powder

No-cook fudge candy hides a crunchy nut in the centre. Boxed or bagged, these make good presents, too!

1) In a large bowl, sift the icing sugar and cocoa powder. Using a baking spatula, stir in the milk powder (don't sift this ingredient). Mix well and set aside.

2) In a microwave-safe bowl, heat the butter, water, and vanilla in the microwave at 50% power until the butter is melted (about 30 seconds). Use the baking spatula to scrape the butter mixture into the icing sugar mixture. Stir until it gets too stiff to mix, then use your hands to squeeze it into a smooth fudge-like "dough." Use a dinner knife to scrape sticky ingredients off the spatula. The "dough" should be soft but not sticky. No dry icing sugar should be left.

3) To make a Hazelnut Fudge Pebble, press the fudge firmly into a measuring teaspoon until the spoon is filled level. Push the fudge out of the spoon with your finger and flatten it slightly. Place a nut into the middle, then squeeze the fudge around the nut to seal it tightly (you should not be able to see the nut) and roll into a ball. Make up to 22 balls, using up all the fudge.

4) Sift the last 2 tbsp cocoa powder into a bowl. Roll the fudge balls, one or two at a time, in the cocoa to coat them. Hold the fudge balls loosely in your cupped hand and shake off the loose cocoa. Place them on a plate and chill them for 15 minutes to firm up before eating. After chilling once, the pebbles hold their shape perfectly at room temperature. If you plan to give these as gifts, keep them chilled until you box them up.

Makes up to 22 Hazelnut Fudge Pebbles.

HAZELNUT FUDGE PEBBLES

Double-Chocolate Brownies

SUPPLIES

pastry brush or cling film; 20 cm square glass, ceramic, or metal baking tin, sieve, measuring spoons, bowls, measuring cups, microwavable food cover, heatproof baking spatula, whisk, wooden spoon, soup spoon, dinner knife; if frosting: baking spatula or palette knife

INGREDIENTS

soft butter for baking tin

1 tsp unsweetened cocoa powder for baking tin

3 squares (30 g each) unsweetened chocolate

125 ml (½ cup) unsalted butter

160 ml (⅔ cup) packed brown sugar

125 ml (½ cup) white sugar

1 tbsp unsweetened cocoa powder

1 tbsp vegetable oil

½ tsp vanilla extract

160 ml (⅔ cup) plain flour (spoon in, level; see page 19)

2 eggs

4 tbsp chocolate chips

Classic Brownie or Mint Brownie Frosting, if you like (see page 203)

One of the most popular recipes from the original *Kids Kitchen* cookbook is the Classic Brownies, the perfect cakey-fudgy treats. This version has extra chocolate!

1. Preheat the oven to 180°C/160°C fan/gas 4.

2. Use a pastry brush or a scrunched-up piece of cling film to rub the bottom and sides of the baking tin with butter. Then sift 1 tsp cocoa powder into the tin. Tip the baking tin around to roll the cocoa over the bottom so it sticks to the butter. This will help keep the brownies from sticking to the tin. Set aside.

3. Put the chocolate squares and the unsalted butter into a large microwave-safe bowl. Cover the bowl with a microwavable food cover, if you have one (it prevents larger amounts of melting butter from splattering). Heat in the microwave at 50% power for 1 minute at a time, two or three times, until the chocolate and butter are melted. After each minute, poke the chocolate with a baking spatula to check if it has melted—melted squares of chocolate hold their shape until stirred. Get help removing the hot bowl from the microwave.

4. Use the baking spatula to stir the chocolate and butter until smooth. Set aside.

5. Put the brown sugar, white sugar, and cocoa powder in a separate bowl. Use the end of a whisk or the back of a wooden spoon to mash out any lumps in the brown sugar and cocoa powder.

6. Add the sugar/cocoa mixture to the melted chocolate and butter.

7. Add the oil and vanilla to the chocolate mixture. Mix well. Set aside to cool.

8. Meanwhile, put the flour into a bowl. Set aside.

CONTINUED ON PAGE 202

DOUBLE-CHOCOLATE BROWNIES WITH
MINT BROWNIE FROSTING (PAGE 203)

Double-Chocolate Brownies (cont'd)

(9) Check that the chocolate mixture has cooled to lukewarm. Use a whisk to mix in the eggs until smooth.

(10) Use a soup spoon to gradually add a few heaped spoonfuls of flour at a time to the chocolate mixture. Mix well with the baking spatula. Use a dinner knife to scrape sticky ingredients from the spatula. Stir in the chocolate chips. Scrape the batter into the baking tin, spreading evenly. Clean off the spatula again with the dinner knife.

(11) Bake for 23 to 25 minutes, until the top is set but the brownies are still soft in the middle. Do not over-bake or the brownies will not be fudgy. Cool completely in the tin before using a baking spatula or palette knife to spread Classic Brownie or Mint Brownie Frosting overtop, if you like. To keep brownies at their moistest, leave them in the tin and slice off squares as you serve them.

Makes 16 Double-Chocolate Brownies.

CLASSIC BROWNIE FROSTING [GF]

A rich frosting that tastes like a layer of chocolate fudge on the brownies.

SUPPLIES

bowls, measuring spoons, sieve, measuring cup, baking spatula, dinner knife, ordinary teaspoon

INGREDIENTS

3 tbsp unsalted butter

2 tbsp milk, plus a few drops
  more if needed

250 ml (1 cup) icing sugar (spoon in,
  level; see page 19)

3 tbsp unsweetened cocoa powder

pinch of salt

¼ tsp vanilla extract

1. In a large bowl, heat the butter and milk in the microwave at 50% power until the butter is melted (about 1 minute). Get help taking the bowl out of the microwave.

2. In another large bowl, sift the icing sugar, cocoa powder, and salt. Mix well with a baking spatula.

3. Use an ordinary teaspoon to gradually add spoonfuls of the icing sugar mixture into the butter mixture, stirring with the baking spatula after each addition. After all the icing sugar mixture has been added, stir in the vanilla. Use a dinner knife to scrape sticky ingredients off the spatula.

4. If the frosting is too thick to spread, stir in a few drops of milk. If it's too runny, stir in a spoonful of sifted icing sugar. Spread on cooled brownies. Let stand a few minutes to set.

Makes enough frosting to cover one 20 cm square tin of brownies.

PICTURED ON PAGE 205

MINT BROWNIE FROSTING [GF]

Mint and chocolate taste wonderful together. Try it!

SUPPLIES

bowl, measuring spoons, sieve, measuring cup, baking spatula, dinner knife

INGREDIENTS

2 tbsp unsalted butter

1 tbsp milk

375 ml (1½ cups) icing sugar (spoon in,
  level; see page 19)

pinch of salt

¼ tsp peppermint extract

⅛ tsp vanilla extract

2 drops green food colouring, if you wish

1. In a large microwave-safe bowl, heat the butter and milk in the microwave at 50% power until the butter is melted (about 30 seconds). Get help removing the bowl from the microwave.

2. Sift the icing sugar into the bowl of milk and butter. Use a baking spatula to stir until smooth. Use a dinner knife to scrape sticky ingredients off the spatula. It will look like there's too much icing sugar at first, but keep stirring and the sugar will melt down.

3. Stir in the salt, peppermint extract, vanilla, and green food colouring, if using. If the frosting is too thick to spread, stir in a few more drops of milk until creamy. If it's not thick enough, sift in another heaped spoonful of icing sugar and stir in. Spread on cooled brownies. Before slicing, let the brownies stand until the frosting is no longer sticky.

Makes enough frosting to cover one 20 cm square tin of brownies.

PICTURED ON PAGE 201

Fudgelicious Brownies

[GF]

SUPPLIES

pastry brush or cling film, 20 cm
square glass, ceramic, or metal
baking tin, sieve, measuring spoons,
measuring cups, bowls, microwavable
food cover, baking spatula, whisk,
dinner knife; if frosting: baking spatula
or palette knife

INGREDIENTS

soft butter for baking tin

1 tsp unsweetened cocoa powder for
baking tin

330 ml (1⅓ cups) semi-sweet chocolate
chips

5 tbsp unsalted butter

5 tbsp unsweetened cocoa powder
(spoon in, level; see page 19)

3 tbsp cornflour

5 tbsp packed brown sugar

2 tbsp white sugar

pinch of salt

125 ml (½ cup) unsweetened apple
sauce

1 tsp vanilla extract

2 eggs

Classic Brownie or Mint Brownie
Frosting, if you like (see page 203)

These beauties are so delectably moist, you could
even eat them without frosting. Check that your
chips and cocoa powder are gluten-free.

(1) Preheat the oven to 170°C/150°C fan/gas 3.

(2) Use a pastry brush or a scrunched-up piece of cling film to
butter the bottom and sides of the baking tin. Sift 1 tsp cocoa
powder into the tin. Tip the tin around to roll the cocoa over
the bottom (you don't need to coat the sides with cocoa). This
stops the brownies from sticking in the tin. Set aside.

(3) Put the chocolate chips and 5 tbsp butter in a large microwave-
safe bowl. Cover the bowl with a microwavable food cover,
if you have one. Heat in the microwave at 50% power for 1
minute at a time, two or three times, until the chocolate chips
and butter are melted. After each minute, poke the chocolate
chips with a baking spatula to check if they've melted. Get help
removing the hot bowl from the microwave. Use the baking
spatula to stir the chocolate and butter until smooth. Set aside
to cool slightly.

(4) Meanwhile, in another large bowl, sift the 5 tbsp cocoa powder
and cornflour. Use a whisk to stir in the brown sugar (break up
any lumps), white sugar, and salt. Set aside.

(5) Go back to the bowl of melted butter and chocolate. Check that
it's lukewarm, not hot. Use the whisk to stir in the apple sauce
and vanilla until smooth. Then stir in the eggs until smooth.

(6) Pour the dry mixture into the wet mixture. Stir with the whisk
into a smooth batter. Use the baking spatula to scrape it evenly
into the baking dish. Clean off the spatula with a dinner knife.

(7) Bake on the middle rack of the oven for 40 minutes, until the
top is set but the brownies are still soft. Cool completely in the
tin before using a baking spatula or palette knife to spread with
Classic Brownie or Mint Brownie Frosting, if you like.

Makes 16 Fudgelicious Brownies.

FUDGELICIOUS BROWNIES WITH
CLASSIC BROWNIE FROSTING (PAGE 203)

Custards in a Warm Bath

[GF]

SUPPLIES

bowls, heatproof baking spatula, measuring cups, measuring spoons, six 125 ml oven-proof ramekins or custard cups (or five 160 ml ramekins or custard cups), roasting pan or large baking dish, whisk, 500 ml liquid measuring jug

INGREDIENTS

250 ml milk

250 ml whipping cream

5 tbsp white sugar

½ tsp vanilla extract

pinch of salt

4 eggs

4 tbsp firmly packed brown sugar

3 tbsp water

The fancy name for these sweet, silky egg custards is crème caramel. They're baked in a "bath" of water to keep them soft and moist. They're good eaten warm or chilled.

1. Preheat the oven to 170°C/150°C fan/gas 3.

2. In a large microwave-safe bowl, use a heatproof baking spatula to mix the milk, whipping cream, white sugar, vanilla and salt. Heat in the microwave on high for 1 minute. Get help taking the bowl out of the microwave. Gently stir the mixture to start melting the sugar. Microwave again on high for another minute (do not microwave for more than a minute at a time or the mixture could foam over). It is important to melt all the sugar. Microwave one or two more times, stirring in between, until the sugar is completely dissolved. Set aside to cool to lukewarm.

3. Set the five or six ramekins or custard cups in a roasting tin or large baking dish.

4. Crack the four eggs into a big bowl. Use a whisk to beat them until the whites and yolks are blended.

5. Check if the milk mixture is lukewarm or barely warm—if it's still too hot, wait a little longer for it to cool down.

6. Use a 500 ml measuring jug to scoop about 125 ml of the lukewarm milk mixture and whisk it into the eggs. Then pour the rest of the egg mixture into the milk mixture. Whisk until blended. This is the custard mixture.

7. Ask a helper to help you pour equal amounts of the custard mixture into the ramekins or custard cups. Or, if you want to fill the ramekins or custard cups, ask your helper to pour some custard mixture into the measuring jug for you first. The helper can refill this pouring cup for you as you fill the ramekins or custard cups.

(8) Rinse out the jug and use it to add warm tap water into the roasting pan or large baking dish—but don't get water in the custards! Add enough warm water to reach half way up the outside of the ramekins or custard cups.

(9) Get help putting the pan of custards in the oven. Bake for 40 to 45 minutes, until the custards are set. Get help removing the pan from the oven. Let cool until lukewarm, about 10 minutes.

(10) Meanwhile, make the brown-sugar syrup by mixing the brown sugar and 3 tbsp water in a clean, microwave-safe bowl and heating it in the microwave on high for 45 seconds. Get help removing the bowl from the microwave. Use a clean baking spatula to stir until the brown sugar is dissolved. You might need to heat it again for 30 seconds to melt the sugar.

(11) Spoon the brown sugar syrup onto the five or six baked custards. Eat while warm, or cool down and then chill for several hours or overnight to serve cold.

Makes 5 or 6 Custards in a Warm Bath.

CUSTARDS IN A WARM BATH

Tirami-Moo

SUPPLIES

dinner knife, bowls, measuring cups, wooden spoon, whisk, measuring spoons, baking spatula, 23 × 12cm glass, ceramic, or metal loaf tin, shallow dish, sieve

INGREDIENTS

125 g cream cheese

4 tbsp white sugar

125 ml milk

¼ tsp vanilla extract

125 ml milk

4 tbsp instant vanilla pudding powder (not the kind that needs cooking)

250 ml plain or chocolate milk

12 to 14 savoiardi biscuits (crisp ladyfinger cookies)

160 ml whipped cream or topping (this is *already* whipped)

½ tsp unsweetened cocoa powder

A kids' version of the Italian dessert tiramisu. The cookies are dipped into milk, not coffee, to soften. No baking is required, but you do need to chill this dish for several hours.

(1) Use a dinner knife to cut the block of cream cheese into eight or nine big pieces. Put them in a large microwave-safe bowl and heat in the microwave at 50% power to soften (about 1 minute). Use the back of a wooden spoon to cream in the sugar.

(2) Stir 125 ml of milk into the cream cheese mixture. Just roughly mix it in; it will not blend in completely yet. Put the bowl back in the microwave and heat again at 50% power for 1 minute. Switch to a whisk and mix smooth. Whisk in the vanilla extract, another 125 ml of milk, and the instant pudding mix. Mix smooth. This is the vanilla custard.

(3) Use a baking spatula or wooden spoon to spread about half the custard evenly in the bottom of the loaf tin.

(4) Put the 250 ml of milk into a shallow dish. Roll one savoiardi biscuit at a time into the milk. It will soften right away, so you should work pretty quickly so the cookies don't get too soft to hold. Lay the dipped biscuits touching side by side on the custard in the loaf tin. Gently press them into the custard. Try not to leave gaps between the biscuits. It's okay to break some cookies into pieces to fill in spaces. Use about half the biscuits in this layer.

(5) Spread the rest of the custard on top of the row of cookies. Dip the rest of the biscuits—one at a time—in the milk and place them in another row on the top layer of custard.

(6) Use a clean baking spatula to spread the whipped cream or topping evenly overtop.

(7) Put the cocoa powder into the sieve. Hold it about 12 cm over the loaf tin and tap the edge of the sieve to sprinkle cocoa powder evenly on top. Chill for at least 3 hours or overnight. Slice to serve. Store any leftovers in the refrigerator.

Serves 8.

TIRAMI-MOO

Cheesecake Mousse and Cookie Parfaits

SUPPLIES

dinner knife, bowls, measuring cups,
wooden spoon, measuring spoons,
drinking cup, ordinary teaspoon,
baking spatula, whisk, 6 small glasses
(about 185 ml each)

INGREDIENTS

125 g cream cheese

5 tbsp + 1 tbsp
white sugar

3 tbsp warm tap water

2 tsp unflavoured gelatin powder

125 ml vanilla yogurt
(or 125 ml plain yogurt plus ¼ tsp
vanilla extract)

250 ml whipped cream or topping (this
is *already* whipped)

250 ml (1 cup) fresh blueberries

18 vanilla wafer cookies (small round
cookies, 4 cm wide)

Individual no-bake, chilled desserts that taste like fluffy cheesecake with fresh fruit.

1. Use a dinner knife to cut the cream cheese into eight or nine pieces. Put them into a large microwave-safe bowl and heat in the microwave at 50% power to soften (about 1 minute). Use the back of a wooden spoon to cream in the sugar. Set aside.

2. Measure the warm tap water into a drinking cup. Add the gelatin powder and stir with an ordinary teaspoon. Pour the gelatin and water into the cream cheese mixture. Use a baking spatula to scrape all the bits of gelatin clinging to the glass into the cream cheese mixture. Use a whisk to stir smooth.

3. Still using the whisk, stir the vanilla yogurt (or plain yogurt and vanilla extract) into the cream cheese mixture until smooth.

4. Use a baking spatula to fold the whipped cream or topping into the cream cheese mixture. Folding means to gently mix ingredients without squishing out the air. Add the whipped cream or topping onto the cream cheese mixture in the bowl. Slice the blade of the baking spatula around the whipped cream and under the cream cheese mixture, going in big circles down to the bottom of the bowl and back up again, until the ingredients are blended but still fluffy. This is the cheesecake mousse.

5. Using a clean ordinary teaspoon, drop a heaped spoonful of the mousse into each glass. Top each glass with four or five blueberries, a cookie, followed by another spoonful of mousse, then another four or five blueberries. Use up all the mousse.

6. Finish by sticking two vanilla wafer cookies on top of each glass of mousse. To do this, hold the cookies as if you are dropping coins into a piggy bank and stick them into the mousse until they are halfway hidden. Chill the cups for at least two hours or overnight before eating. Store any leftovers in the refrigerator.

Makes 6 Cheesecake Mousse and Cookie Parfaits.

CHEESECAKE MOUSSE AND
COOKIE PARFAITS

index

a

Almond-Oat Baked Apples, 179

apples

    Almond-Oat Baked Apples, 179

    Apple Crisp, 182

    Fruit Fritters, 185

Apricot Scoop Cake, 119

b

Bacon!, Good Morning, 24

baking tins, 13

baking racks, 14, 17

baking sheets, 15

bananas

    Chocolate Banana Loaf, 105–106

    Cocoa-Kissed Banana Oatmeal, 63

    Fruit Fritters, 185

    Rainy Day Banana Bread, 114

    Warm Caramel Banana Sundaes, 186

BBQ-Sauced Chicken, Your Own, 59

beef

    Beef Stew Ooh-La-La, 47

    Lovin' Oven Hamburgers, 76

Berry Shortcakes, Fresh, 188

Biscuits, Baker's Dozen Chive, 35

blueberries

    Blueberry Sunshine Muffins, 116

    Cheesecake Mousse and Cookie Parfaits, 210

    Little Fresh Blueberry Pies, 109–111

bowls, 13

breads

    Burger Buns, 78–79

    Champion Ciabatta, 136–137

    Cheddar Egg Bread, 140–141

    Chocolate Banana Loaf, 105–106

    Feta Focaccia Bread, 134

    French Toast in a Pan, 22

    Soft Twisted Pepperoni Breadsticks, 88–89

    Spring Onion Bread, 143

    Tomato Salsa Cornbread, 142

    Warm Chocolate Brioches, 107–108

    Whole Wheat Sandwich Bread, 138–139

Brioches, Warm Chocolate, 107–108

brownies

    Double-Chocolate Brownies, 200–202

    Fudgelicious Brownies, 204

burgers

    Burger Buns, 78–79

    Gobble-Up Turkey Burgers, 74

    Lovin' Oven Hamburgers, 76

butter, 13, 16

Buttercream Frosting, Cocoa, 124

c

cakes. see also frosting; glazes

    Apricot Scoop Cake, 119

    Cheesecake Mousse and Cookie Parfaits, 210

    Dark Chocolate Cake, 133

    Fresh Berry Shortcakes, 188

    Fresh Lemon Cupcakes, 100

    Little Black Forest Cake, 120–121

    Pink Cherry Cake, 122

    Surprising Chocolate Cake, 127

    Vanilla Velvet Cake, 128

Caramel Banana Sundaes, Warm, 186

Carrots, Cinnamon Baby, 33

Cashew Couscous (Bless You!), 27

cheese

    Cheddar Egg Bread, 140–141

    Cheese Pizza Muffins, 144

    Feta Focaccia Bread, 134

    Hocus Pocus Pizza, 72–73

    Hula Hawaiian Pizza, 70–71

    Mozzarella Chicken, 52

    Parmesan Puffs, 96

    Parmesan Risotto, 41

pre-grated, 18

Real Mac 'n' Cheddar Cheese, 66

Roasted Tomato and Bocconcini Salad, 28

Warm Caramel Banana Sundaes, 186

Whoopie Pies, 190

Cheesecake Mousse and Cookie Parfaits, 210

Cherry Cake, Pink, 122

chicken

Coconut-Curry Kookoo Chicken, 48

Mozzarella Chicken, 52

Really Big Chicken Meatballs, 83

Tangy Chicken Wings, 86–87

Unfried Picnic Chicken Drumsticks, 44

Your Own BBQ-Sauced Chicken, 59

Chips, Tortilla Corn, 93–95

Chive Biscuits, Baker's Dozen, 35

chocolate

Chocolate Banana Loaf, 105–106

Chocolate Chippers, 149

Chocolate Rondelles, 173

Classic Brownie Frosting, 203

Cocoa Buttercream Frosting, 124

Cocoa Cranberry Crack-Ups, 160

Cocoa-Kissed Banana Oatmeal, 63

Cookie Tortoises, 167

Dark Chocolate Cake, 133

Dark Chocolate Crisps, 163

Double-Chocolate Brownies, 200–202

Frosting Fudge, 131

Fudgelicious Brownies, 204

Fudgy Frosting, 130

Hazelnut Fudge Pebbles, 198

Little Black Forest Cake, 120–121

Peek-a-Pokes, 153

Surprising Chocolate Cake, 127

Sweet Date Pockets, 157–159

Tirami-Moo, 208

Warm Chocolate Brioches, 107–108

Whoopie Pies, 190

cinnamon

Cinnamon Baby Carrots, 33

Cinnamoons, 151–152

cocoa powder, 16

Coconut-Curry Kookoo Chicken, 48

cookies

Brown Sugar Crinkles, 174

Chocolate Chippers, 149

Chocolate Rondelles, 173

Cinnamoons, 151–152

Cocoa Cranberry Crack-Ups, 160

Cookie Tortoises, 167

Dark Chocolate Crisps, 163

Finnigans, 164–165

Glossy Cookie Glaze, 156

Nuterettis, 168

Old-Fashioned Sugar Cookies, 154–156

Peanut Butter Beezies, 175

Peek-a-Pokes, 153

Sugar Delights, 170–172

Sweet Date Pockets, 157–159

corn

Tomato Salsa Cornbread, 142

Tortilla Corn Chips, 93–95

cornflour, 16

Couscous (Bless You!), Cashew, 27

Crackers, Munchy Crunchy, 90–92

Cranberry Crack-Ups, Cocoa, 160

cream cheese

about, 16

Cheesecake Mousse and Cookie Parfaits, 210

Tirami-Moo, 208

"cream" ingredients, 16

Cupcakes, Fresh Lemon, 100

Curry Kookoo Chicken, Coconut-, 48

Custards in a Warm Bath, 206–207

d

dates
  Peek-a-Pokes, 153
  Sweet Date Pockets, 157–159
desserts. *see also* cakes; chocolate; cookies
  Almond-Oat Baked Apples, 179
  Apple Crisp, 182
  Buttery Granola Bars, 197
  Cheesecake Mousse and Cookie Parfaits, 210
  Classic Brownie Frosting, 203
  Custards in a Warm Bath, 206–207
  Double-Chocolate Brownies, 200–202
  Fresh Berry Shortcakes, 188
  Fruit Fritters, 185
  Fudgelicious Brownies, 204
  Hazelnut Fudge Pebbles, 198
  Mint Brownie Frosting, 203
  Peaches in Pastry Nests, 180–181
  Sponge Toffee Lollipops, 193–195
  Sugared Doughnut Puffs, 103–104
  Tirami-Moo, 208
  Warm Caramel Banana Sundaes, 186
  Whoopie Pie Filling, 192
  Whoopie Pies, 190
Doughnut Puffs, Sugared, 103–104
drinking cups, 16

e

eggs
  about, 16
  Cheddar Egg Bread, 140–141
  French Toast in a Pan, 22
  Fruit Fritters, 185
  Spinach and Mushroom Frittata, 69

f

Filling, Whoopie Pie, 192
fish
  Fin-Tastic Fish Fillets, 80
  Seven Seas Salmon, 55
flour, rice, 18
"fold" ingredients, 16
Frittata, Spinach and Mushroom, 69

frosting

  Classic Brownie Frosting, 203
  Cocoa Buttercream Frosting, 124
  Fudgy Frosting, 130
  Mint Brownie Frosting, 203
  Pink Cloud Frosting, 124
  tips, 125
  Vanilla Cream Frosting, 130
fudge
  Frosting Fudge, 131
  Fudgelicious Brownies, 204
  Hazelnut Fudge Pebbles, 198

g

garlic powder, 17
garlic salt, 17
glazes
  Fresh Lemon Double-Glaze, 102
  Glossy Cookie Glaze, 156
  O.J. Glaze, 115
  Tangy Chicken Wings, 86–87
glossary, 15–19
gluten-free, 17
gluten-free icon, 5
Granola Bars, Buttery, 197
Green Beans, Buttered, 40

h

ham: Hula Hawaiian Pizza, 70–71
hazelnuts
  Hazelnut Fudge Pebbles, 198
  Nuterettis, 168

i

ice cream: Warm Caramel Banana Sundaes, 186

k

kitchen utensils/equipment
  baking tins, 13
  baking racks, 14
  baking sheets, 15
  bowls, 13
  drinking cups, 16

knives, 16

microwave ovens, 14

parchment paper, 17

pizza wheel, 18

sieves, 18

spatulas, 15

teaspoons, 17

whisks, 19

knives, 16

l

lemons

Fresh Lemon Cupcakes, 100

Fresh Lemon Double-Glaze, 102

Lettuce Wraps with Crumbled Asian Pork, 85

loaves

Chocolate Banana Loaf, 105–106

Rainy Day Banana Bread, 114

Lollipops, Sponge Toffee, 193–195

m

marinades: Tangy Chicken Wings, 86–87

masa harina, 17

measuring dry ingredients, 13–14

measuring wet ingredients, 14

Meatballs, Really Big Chicken, 83

microwave ovens, 14

Mint Brownie Frosting, 203

Mousse and Cookie Parfaits, Cheesecake, 210

muffins

Blueberry Sunshine Muffins, 116

Cheese Pizza Muffins, 144

Mushroom Frittata, Spinach and, 69

o

oats

Almond-Oat Baked Apples, 179

Buttery Granola Bars, 197

Cocoa-Kissed Banana Oatmeal, 63

onion powder, 17

onion salt, 17

oranges: O.J. Glaze, 115

p

parchment paper, 17

Parfaits, Cheesecake Mousse and Cookie, 210

pasta

Lasagne Jumble, 51

Real Mac 'n' Cheddar Cheese, 66

Rice, Orzo, and Split Pea Trio, 43

Peaches in Pastry Nests, 180–181

peanut butter

Cookie Tortoises, 167

Peanut Butter Beezies, 175

peas

Rice, Orzo, and Split Pea Trio, 43

Simple Rice and Peas, 32

Pecan Sweetie Pies, 112

pepperoni

Hocus Pocus Pizza, 72–73

Soft Twisted Pepperoni Breadsticks, 88–89

pies

Little Fresh Blueberry Pies, 109–111

Pecan Sweetie Pies, 112

Whoopie Pies, 190

pizza

Cheese Pizza Muffins, 144

Hocus Pocus Pizza, 72–73

Hula Hawaiian Pizza, 70–71

wheel, 18

pork

Every-Flavour Pork Chops, 56

Lettuce Wraps with Crumbled Asian Pork, 85

potatoes

Smashed Mini Potatoes, 36

starch, 18

Upside-Down Baked Potatoes, 38

r

raspberries: Warm Caramel Banana Sundaes, 186

rice

Feast Rice, 31

flour, 18

Parmesan Risotto, 41

rice (continued)

    Rice, Orzo, and Split Pea Trio, 43

    Simple Rice and Peas, 32

ricotta cheese

    Fresh Berry Shortcakes, 188

    Whoopie Pies, 190

Risotto, Parmesan, 41

S

Salad, Roasted Tomato and Bocconcini, 28

Salmon, Seven Seas, 55

salt, 18

Sausages, Batch o' Brekkie, 26

Shortcakes, Fresh Berry, 188

sieves, 19

spatulas, 15

Spinach and Mushroom Frittata, 69

Sponge Toffee Lollipops, 193–195

Spring Onion Bread, 143

"spoon in, level," 19

Stew Ooh-La-La, Beef, 47

strawberries

    Fresh Berry Shortcakes, 188

    Warm Caramel Banana Sundaes, 186

Sundaes, Warm Caramel Banana, 186

t

tapioca starch, 19

teaspoons, 17

Toffee Lollipops, Sponge, 193–195

tomatoes

    Roasted Tomato and Bocconcini Salad, 28

    Tomato Salsa Cornbread, 142

Turkey Burgers, Gobble-Up, 74

V

vanilla

    Vanilla Cream Frosting, 130

    Vanilla Velvet Cake, 128

W

walnuts: Cookie Tortoises, 167

whipped cream, 19

whisks, 19

Wraps with Crumbled Asian Pork, Lettuce, 85

y

yeast, 19

yogurt

    Cheesecake Mousse and Cookie Parfaits, 210

    Fin-tastic Fish Fillets, 80

    Unfried Picnic Chicken Drumsticks, 44